THE
HORSE
THE FOOT, SHOEING
& LAMENESS

THE
HORSE
THE FOOT, SHOEING & LAMENESS

Julie Brega

J.A. Allen
London

British Library Cataloguing in Publication Data
A catalogue record for this book is available from the British Library

ISBN 0.85131.612.3

Published in Great Britain in 1995 by
J. A. Allen and Company Limited,
1 Lower Grosvenor Place,
Buckingham Palace Road,
London, SW1W 0EL.

Typeset in Hong Kong by Setrite Typesetters Ltd.
Printed in Hong Kong by Dah Hua Printing Press Co. Ltd.

CONTENTS

LIST OF
ILLUSTRATIONS

ix

ACKNOWLEDGEMENTS

I would like to thank the following friends for their invaluable help in the production of this book:

Debby Baker, for deciphering and typesetting the original manuscript.

Annalisa Barrelet, BVetMed, MS, Cert ESM, MRCVS, for veterinary editing and much expert advice.

Kitty Best, for the excellent illustrations.

Martin Diggle, for his patience and editing skills.

Stuart Marshall, DWCF for help and advice on the farriery aspects.

   And special thanks to my family:
To my parents, John and Sheila Hollywood, who look after our children, Holly and Josh, so brilliantly, allowing me to get some work done, to my step-daughter, Zoe, for keeping the horses, office and myself organized, and finally to my husband, Bill, for his constant help and support.

INTRODUCTION

The Horse: The Foot, Shoeing and Lameness is one of six books in the Progressive Series. This series forms the basis of an advanced open learning course offered by The Open College of Equestrian Studies.

The main objective of these books is to present the information needed by the equestrian enthusiast in a clear and logical manner. This information is invaluable to everyone interested in horses, whether in a professional capacity as a yard manager or examination trainee, or as a private horse-owner.

Shoeing and lameness are vast specialist subjects. Vets and farriers train for several years and research continues into the many causes and treatments of various types of lameness. While this book is not intended to replace the advice of the vet or farrier, it will give the horse manager an insight into many different aspects of the subjects. A well-informed owner or manager will be more likely to prevent a problem from occurring in the first place and, in the event of one arising, will be better able to deal with it. Discussions with the vet or farrier will also be more meaningful.

Before shoeing and lameness can be understood, it is necessary to be familiar with the structures of the foot and lower leg. Therefore, the first section of this book deals with the anatomy of the foot; the structures, their composition and functions. This is followed by the daily and long-term care of the feet, including shoeing. Corrective and therapeutic shoes are then discussed.

The next major heading is 'Lameness'. Covered here is the process of examining a lame horse to determine which leg is affected. Under 'Causes of Lameness' the causes, signs and treatment of the various ailments affecting the leg and foot are explained. These ailments range from nail bind to navicular, laminitis to limb fracture.

Because many lamenesses have associated inflammation, the next section of the book explains the different anti-inflammatory therapies available. These range from simple procedures such as hosing and tubbing, to more sophisticated techniques such as ultrasound and laser. During any period of recovery from lameness, it is important to plan a rehabilitation programme appropriate to the horse's needs. Recovery and rehabilitation therefore conclude this book.

The overall conclusion is that it is the responsibility of everyone who rides and looks after horses to understand the workings of the horse's lower leg, so that they can take care on a day-to-day basis to promote the long-term soundness of the horse.

1

THE ANATOMY OF THE FOOT

As riders become more competitive and demand greater levels of fitness to be maintained for longer periods, horses and ponies are placed under ever-increasing strain. The resultant stresses, which will ultimately be passed onto the bones, joints, ligaments and tendons of equine limbs, may sometimes prove too great, resulting in detrimental changes taking place. Therefore, good management is needed if the competition horse is to stay sound throughout his career. While it is the farrier who provides the basis of such management, it is important that the owner has a knowledge of the anatomy of the horse's limbs so that he or she can understand the reasoning behind the farrier's decision to shoe the horse in any particular manner when trying to prevent or treat problems.

THE BONES OF THE FOOT

The long pastern

Sometimes referred to as the first phalanx, this bone extends downwards and forwards from the fetlock joint. It assumes an oblique position and should be at the same angle to the ground as the line of the hoof wall: 45–50 degrees in the forelimbs; 50–55 degrees in the hind limbs. If the long pastern is very

1

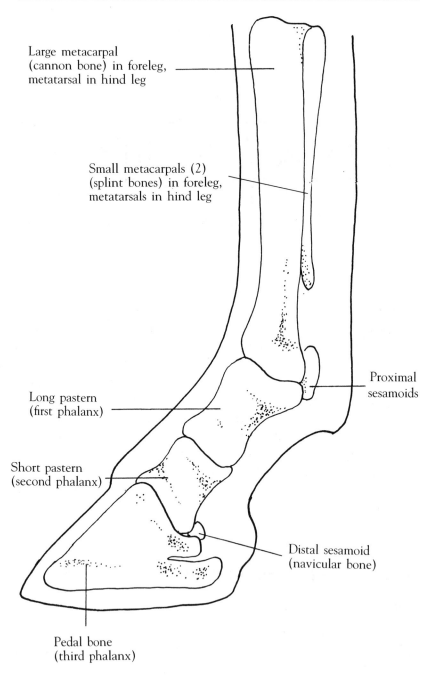

Large metacarpal (cannon bone) in foreleg, metatarsal in hind leg

Small metacarpals (2) (splint bones) in foreleg, metatarsals in hind leg

Proximal sesamoids

Long pastern (first phalanx)

Short pastern (second phalanx)

Distal sesamoid (navicular bone)

Pedal bone (third phalanx)

Figure 1 The bones of the lower leg (lateral view) and explanation of terminology (opposite)

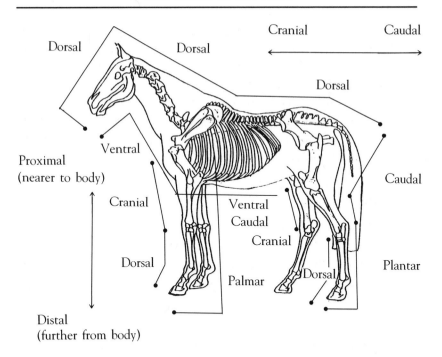

Cranial   Caudal

Dorsal

Dorsal

Dorsal

Dorsal

Proximal
(nearer to body)

Ventral

Cranial   Caudal

Ventral

Caudal

Cranial

Dorsal   Plantar

Dorsal

Palmar

Distal
(further from body)

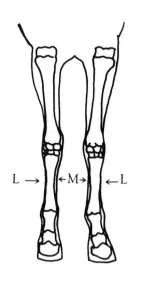

L → ←M→ ←L

L = Lateral

M = Medial

upright it will bear more weight directly and this may render the limb more prone to concussion-related ailments. However, should it slope excessively, extra strain will be placed upon the tendons, ligaments and fetlock joint.

The anterior (front) surface of the long pastern is smooth and slightly rounded while its posterior (rear) surface is flattened and has a roughened area to facilitate attachment of the sesamoidean ligament.

The short pastern

This cube-shaped bone is also referred to as the second phalanx and articulates with the long pastern bone to form the pastern joint. When the horse is standing, the two pastern bones should be at the same angle as the hoof wall, forming a straight 'pastern/foot' axis.

The pedal bone

The distal (lower) surface of the short pastern meets the pedal bone to form the coffin or pedal joint. The pedal bone is also known as the third phalanx or coffin bone and is crescent shaped, corresponding with the shape of the hoof.

The pedal bone is composed of compact, dense bone which, whilst light and porous, makes it very strong and able to withstand great pressure. The bone is pierced by many small holes, known as foramina, which allow the passage of blood vessels.

The dorsal or front (laminal) surface slopes downwards and forwards at an angle of 45−50 degrees to the ground. This surface extends laterally to form the wings, where the height gradually reduces and the angle increases, becoming steeper. Each wing has a horizontal notch known as a preplantar groove through which the preplantar artery passes.

Attached to the upper borders of the wings are the large, elastic, lateral cartilages. These extend above the coronet and may be felt in that region. Whilst allowing expansion of the foot, the lateral cartilages contain and support the digital cushion and so play an important role in the maintenance of adequate circulation of blood within the foot and lower limb.

The whole of the laminal surface forms an attachment with the sensitive laminae. The common digital extensor tendon attaches to the extensor process of the pedal bone. After passing over the navicular bursa, the deep digital flexor tendon attaches to the palmar aspect of the pedal bone.

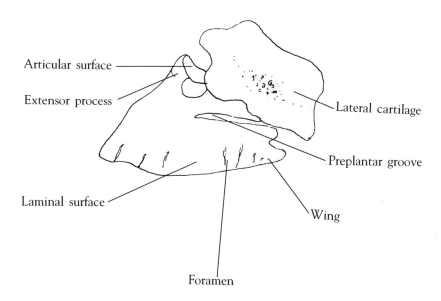

Figure 2 The pedal bone

The navicular bone

To the rear of the coffin joint is the small, transversely elongated navicular bone (sometimes referred to as the distal sesamoid bone). This bone helps to reinforce and strengthen the joint as the foot comes to the ground. The lower surface of the navicular bone is very smooth, being covered in cartilage over which the deep digital flexor tendon glides.

Between the deep digital flexor tendon and the navicular bone is a fluid-filled sac − the navicular bursa. This allows free movement and reduces friction as the tendon passes over the navicular bone.

THE EXTERNAL (INSENSITIVE) STRUCTURES

The hoof wall

The outer, protective layer of the foot, the hoof wall, originates from the horn-secreting tissues of the coronary cushion, a fibro-cartilagenous structure composed of many tiny papillae. These papillae produce the specialized skin cells which form the horn tubules. Also secreted is a glutinous substance which unites the tubules forming a solid mass — inter-tubular horn. Some of the horn tubules are filled up with broken down horn cells, known as intra-tubular horn.

The horn grows from around the coronary cushion at a rate of approximately 6 mm per month. It takes approximately nine to twelve months to grow from coronet to toe and six months from coronet to heel. As it grows the horn becomes compressed, harder and tougher (keratinized). The horn tends to be tougher and thicker at the toe, more pliable at the heel. Overall, the horn should be tough but not brittle, with a slightly elastic quality. Under normal circumstances, horn contains approximately 25 per cent water. This is drawn from the body fluids as well as being absorbed from the external environment.

There are many factors which will affect the rate at which each individual horse's hooves grow. These include:

Diet. The level of nutrition and balance of nutrients, including water, within the diet.

Condition. Bad health or generally 'run-down' poor condition will have an adverse affect on the growth of horn.

Circulation. The efficiency of the heart and lungs will determine the volume of blood and the oxygen levels within the blood, necessary to nourish the structures within the foot.

Exercise. This increases the heart rate, thus increasing the supply of blood to the foot. As exercise is increased, so too is food — this promotes increased growth.

Environment. Growth is slower in a dry environment, quicker in a wet one.

Above the coronary cushion, lying within the perioplic groove, is the perioplic ring; a smaller cushion of fine papillae which secrete a waterproof, varnish-like horn (the periople) which covers the wall, helping to prevent excessive evaporation of moisture from within.

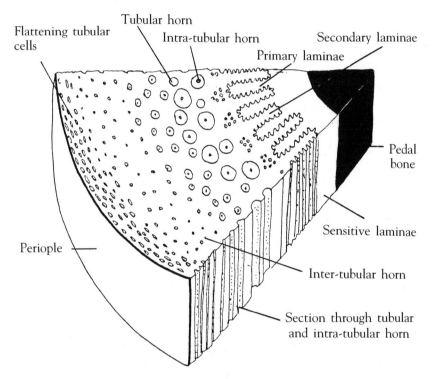

Figure 3 Section through hoof

The horny sole

The sole is a plate of hard horn approximately 2 cm thick. This horn is secreted by papillae from within the sensitive sole and contains approximately 30 per cent water. The sole flakes away in a natural shedding process (exfoliation).

The main functions of the horny sole are to assist in weight carrying and to protect the inner, sensitive structures.

The frog

The insensitive frog appears as a wedge-shaped mass of elastic horn. It is made up of the same type of horn as the wall, but contains more glutinous inter-tubular horn and approximately 40 per cent water, making it the most elastic and pliable structure of the foot.

To either side of the frog and in the centre of its bearing surface are fairly deep clefts, which allow for expansion of the foot.

The frog performs several very important functions, each of which can only be carried out successfully if the frog is in contact with the ground. If the frog does not come into contact with the ground it may become atrophied (diminished) as a result of disuse. The functions of the frog are:

To protect sensitive underlying structures.

To assist in weight carrying; if the frog is not bearing weight, more pressure is borne by the walls of the hoof.

To prevent slipping — the rubbery texture and depression formed by the cleft provide grip.

To protect against concussion. As the foot comes down, the heel touches the ground first, therefore taking the bulk of the weight. This jarring effect is lessened by the rubbery compression of a healthy frog.

To promote a healthy blood supply. The insensitive frog becomes compressed which, in turn, causes pressure on the sensitive frog and digital cushion (see below). This forces the lateral cartilages against the horny wall, which flattens out and empties the blood vessels between the cartilages and wall. Once the pressure is relieved (when the foot is lifted off the ground), the blood vessels refill.

The white line

On the ground surface of the sole, the union between the sole and the wall is marked by a narrow strip consisting of a band of soft, waxy horn called the white line. This soft horn is secreted by papillae on the lower edge of the sensitive laminae and contains approximately 50 per cent water.

THE INTERNAL (SENSITIVE) STRUCTURES

The sensitive frog

This structure is very closely associated with the digital cushion, upon which it is moulded. It is covered with papillae which are responsible for the secretion of horny frog and the nutrition of the digital cushion.

The sensitive sole

This thin layer of tissue corresponds with the horny sole and is composed of a dense network of blood vessels and papillae. The latter secrete the horny sole and supply nutrition to it. The sensitive sole is very firmly attached to the lower surface of the pedal bone.

The digital cushion

This wedge-shaped fibro-elastic pad fills the hollow behind the heels and is of a firm but yielding consistency. Frog pressure compresses the digital cushion which, in turn, causes the expansion of the lateral cartilages as previously described. The digital cushion therefore aids the circulation of blood within the foot as well as helping to reduce concussion. Any blood which is confined within the hoof contributes to the shock-absorbing effect by spreading pressure in a hydraulic manner.

Any factor which affects the expansion of the heels (for example, nails too close to the heels or very tight quarter clips) may have a direct effect upon the circulation within the foot. A lack of movement will also reduce circulation and may lead to fluid-filled limbs and possibly warmth in the area.

The laminae

The hoof is attached to the pedal bone very securely by an interlocking (dovetailing) of hundreds of leaf-like structures known as laminae.

The sensitive or primary laminae. These fleshy, vascular leaves are attached to the periosteum of the laminal surface of the pedal bone, extending downwards from immediately under the coronary cushion to the lower edge of the pedal bone, at which point a fringe of papillae secrete the waxy horn of which the white line is composed.

The horny or secondary laminae. These are thin, flat plates of horn which grow outward from the interior (laminal) surface of the wall and interlock with the sensitive laminae.

The hundreds of laminae provide a very large surface area which helps to distribute the weight of the horse more evenly, thus easing any stress on the pedal bone. It has been calculated that the surface area of the laminae of each foot is approximately $0.74\,\mathrm{m}^2$ (8 sq ft), giving a total bearing surface of $2.97\,\mathrm{m}^2$ (32 sq ft) per horse.

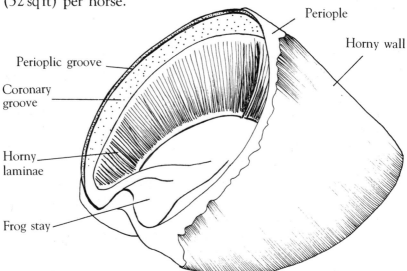

Figure 4(a) Horn structures of the foot (section)

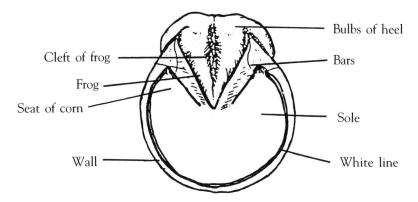

Bulbs of heel

Cleft of frog

Bars

Frog

Seat of corn

Sole

Wall

White line

Figure 4(b) Horn structures of the foot (underside)

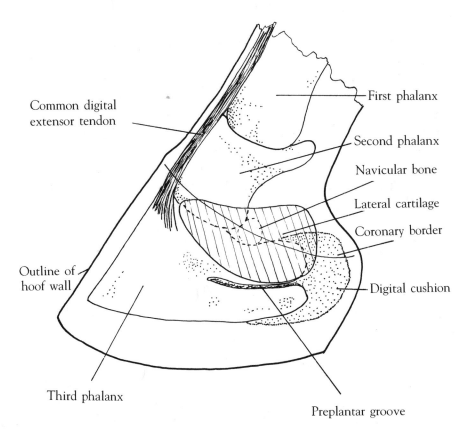

Common digital
extensor tendon

First phalanx

Second phalanx

Navicular bone

Lateral cartilage

Coronary border

Outline of
hoof wall

Digital cushion

Third phalanx

Preplantar groove

Figure 5 Internal structures of the foot

THE VASCULAR SYSTEM OF THE FOOT

The arteries

The common digital artery, which supplies blood to the leg and foot, is also referred to as the large metacarpal artery (forelimbs) and the large metatarsal artery (hind limbs). Running down the metacarpal (metatarsal) bone with the tendons, this artery can sometimes be felt in the hollow immediately above the fetlock joint on the outer aspect. At this point it divides into two; the medial and lateral digital arteries. Separating just above the fetlock joint, these arteries pass either side of the joint, running along the lower edge of the digital flexor tendon and into the inner aspect of the wings of the pedal bone. At this point both arteries subdivide again, into two branches forming the preplantar and plantar arteries.

The preplantar arteries pass through the preplantar grooves on either side of the pedal bone and supply the sensitive laminae and lateral cartilages. The plantar arteries enter the pedal bone through the small holes of the bone, the foramen, and meet in the inner aspect of the pedal bone, the semilunar sinus, to form the terminal arch. From this arch many small branches extend through the foramen, supplying the digital cushion, first and second phalanges, joints, tendons and skin.

The veins

Within the foot there are three distinct networks of veins: the solar venous plexus, the laminal venous plexus and the coronary venous plexus. These intermingle and converge to form the lateral and medial digital veins.

The lateral and medial digital veins ascend the limb in front of their corresponding digital arteries and unite above the fetlock joint between the deep digital flexor tendon and the suspensory ligament to form a venous arch. From this venous arch extend three metacarpal veins: the medial, lateral and deep metacarpals.

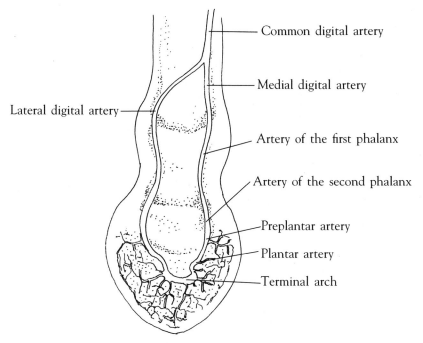

Common digital artery

Medial digital artery

Lateral digital artery

Artery of the first phalanx

Artery of the second phalanx

Preplantar artery

Plantar artery

Terminal arch

Figure 6 The arteries of the foot

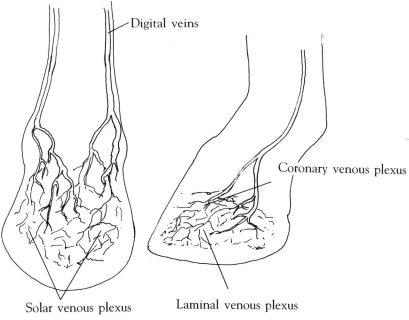

Digital veins

Coronary venous plexus

Solar venous plexus   Laminal venous plexus

Figure 7 The veins of the foot

THE NERVOUS SYSTEM

The lower leg and foot are served by two main nerves and their respective branches. These nerves are the medial and lateral palmar nerves in the foreleg, and the plantar nerves in the hind leg.

The medial palmar nerve

In the foreleg, this nerve is a continuation of the median nerve. It runs down the rear of the cannon bone alongside the superficial digital flexor tendon and large metacarpal artery. Towards the middle of the cannon bone, the nerve branches obliquely over the tendons to join the lateral nerve.

At the fetlock joint, the medial palmar nerve divides into two digital branches. These are:

The dorsal digital branch, which extends forward and divides into two, supplying the skin and hoof.

The palmar digital branch, which descends to the back of the foot, supplying the pedal bone, navicular bone, digital cushion and the tissues of the sole.

The lateral palmar nerve

In the foreleg, this nerve is formed as a result of fusion between the terminal ulna nerve and one of the branches of the median nerve. It descends down the cannon bone, following the line of the deep digital flexor tendon behind the lateral metacarpal vein.

Approximately 2.5 cm (1 in) above the button of the lateral (outside) splint bone, the lateral palmar nerve is joined by a branch of the medial palmar nerve.

At the fetlock joint, the lateral palmar nerve divides into two digital branches which further branch out and supply the medial (inside) aspect of the foot.

The plantar nerves

In the hind leg, the tibial nerve divides, forming the plantar nerves which then descend either side of the deep digital flexor tendon. The medial nerve branches off approximately 2.5 cm (1 in) above the button of the splint bone and joins the lateral nerve. At the fetlock the nerves divide into two and serve the foot as in the forelegs.

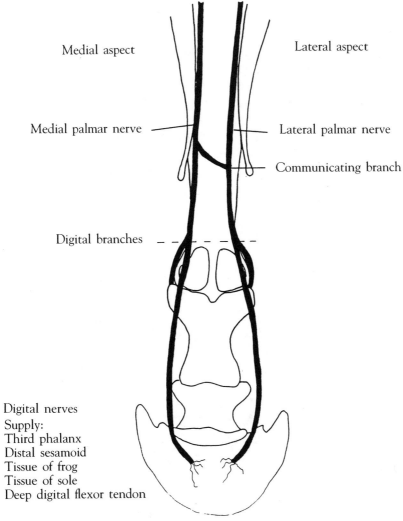

Medial aspect

Lateral aspect

Medial palmar nerve

Lateral palmar nerve

Communicating branch

Digital branches

Digital nerves
Supply:
Third phalanx
Distal sesamoid
Tissue of frog
Tissue of sole
Deep digital flexor tendon

Figure 8 The nerves of the lower leg (palmar/plantar aspect)

THE TENDONS AND LIGAMENTS OF THE LOWER LEG

The tendons

The muscles of the limbs are known as pennate muscles; the fibres of these muscles are short and densely packed, making them very strong. To the belly of each muscle is attached a long tendon. The tendon is well embedded into the belly of the muscle and extends down to the knee, fetlock and digital joints, attaching muscle to the respective bones. There are four tendons in the lower leg; two extensors which are situated dorsally (on the front) and two flexors running down the palmar/plantar (rear) aspect of the limb.

In the region of knee or hock joints, the tendons lie in a groove or canal in the bone. They are covered and held in position by annular ligaments. Annular ligaments are composed of flat bands of connective tissue (fascia).

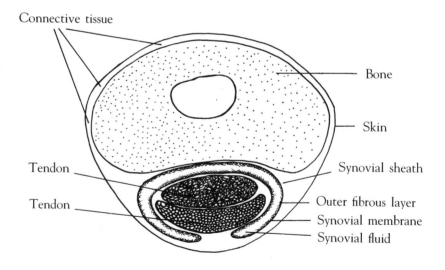

Figure 9 Horizontal cross-section showing synovial tendon sheath

To reduce friction tendons, in some areas, are within a synovial tendon sheath—a double-layered structure, the outer layer of which is in contact with the bone while the inner layer attaches to the tendon. Between the two layers is synovial fluid, which lubricates the tendon.

The extensor tendons

The common digital extensor tendon (CDET) extends down the front of the cannon bone and passes over the fetlock joint, at which point it is reinforced on either side by extensions of the suspensory ligament. These bands also hold the CDET in position. The tendon covers the pastern joint, the short pastern bone and pedal joint before attaching to the upper aspect of the pedal bone. Its function is to extend the lower limb and foot.

The lateral digital extensor tendon (LDET) runs in close proximity with the CDET and inserts into the outer side of the long pastern bone. The LDET helps to straighten and extend the lower leg.

The flexor tendons

The deep digital flexor tendon (DDFT) passes over the back of the knee through the carpal canal, where it is held in position by the flexor retinaculum (a fascia sheet extending down from the flexor muscle). The DDFT is linked to the carpal bones by the carpal check ligament before extending down the back of the cannon bone between the superficial digital flexor tendon and the suspensory ligament. The carpal synovial sheath extends distally to enclose both the deep and superficial digital flexor tendons to the middle of the cannon bone. At this point, the DDFT is joined by its check ligament, the inferior (or carpal) check ligament. The digital synovial sheath surrounds the flexor tendons from a quarter of the way up the cannon bone to midway down the short pastern. The tendon passes over the sesamoid bones, sliding on a glistening pad

formed by the inter-sesamoidean ligament, before passing between the two extensions of the superficial digital flexor tendon.
At this point the DDFT becomes broad and fan-like, passing
over the navicular bone before inserting into the lower surface
of the pedal bone.

The superficial digital flexor tendon (SDFT) passes down the back
of the cannon bone, completely covering the DDFT. At the
upper end of the joint between the long and short pasterns,
The SDFT divides into two branches which insert on the upper
and lower aspects of the short pastern.

The palmar annular ligament binds the SDFT, DDFT and
their tendon sheath to the fetlock joint in the sesamoid groove.
It blends with the SDFT and with the collateral ligaments of
the sesamoid bones.

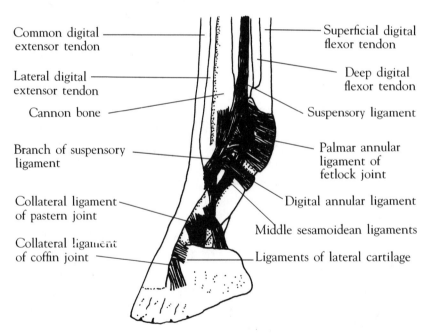

Figure 10 The tendons and ligaments of the lower leg

The ligaments

The function of ligaments is to offer support to joints by attaching one bone firmly to another. The ligaments are named according to their position:

Funicular ligaments are strong, cord-like ligaments attaching bone to bone.

Interosseous ligaments are between adjacent bones, for example between the splint and cannon bones.

Collateral ligaments are of the funicular type and are situated at the side of a joint.

Annular ligaments 'fold' around the tendons to maintain alignment.

The suspensory ligament

This is the longest ligament in the leg. It originates close to the back of the knee and runs downward between the two splint bones towards the fetlock joint, above which it divides into two. Each branch attaches to its corresponding sesamoid bone, with some fibres branching forwards and blending in with the CDET. The main function of the suspensory ligament is to support the fetlock joint, preventing it from overextending downwards, which would result in straining of the flexor tendons.

The check ligaments

The inferior check ligament is below the knee. Its functions are to prevent undue strain being applied to the flexor tendons and to assist in supporting the horse, thus allowing him to sleep while standing. This ligament is connected to the deep flexor tendon.

The superior check ligament is above the knee and connects to the superficial flexor tendon at the back of the humerus. It acts to assist the inferior check ligament.

The sesamoidean ligaments

The sesamoid bones are held in position by three sets of sesamoidean ligaments. These are positioned in layers; superficial, middle and deep. They hold the sesamoid bones to the long pastern bone. The superficial sesamoidean ligaments attach to the upper palmar aspect of the short pastern. The middles attach to the back of the long pastern and the deep ligaments (known as cruciates) cross to attach to the opposite side of the upper aspect of the long pastern.

The collateral sesamoidean ligaments attach the sesamoid bones to the lower aspect of the cannon bone and the top of the long pastern.

Between and slightly above the two sesamoid bones is a mass of fibro-cartilage known as the inter-sesamoidean ligament. In its posterior surface is a groove which accommodates the DDFT.

The ligaments of the fetlock joint

The fetlock joint is supported by two layers of collateral ligaments and a branch of the collateral sesamoidean ligament. The superficial layer of the fetlock's collateral ligaments extends vertically downward from the lower aspect of the cannon bone to a roughened area on the long pastern. The deep layer originates beneath the superficial layer at the bottom of the cannon bone and passes obliquely down and back, attaching to a sesamoid bone and the long pastern.

The ligaments of the pastern joint

The long and short pastern bones are held together by one pair of collateral and two pairs of posterior ligaments, which allow only extension and flexion of the joint — although slight rotation may occur upon manipulation. The collateral ligaments are short, very strong bands which attach to the sides of the long and short pastern bones. Some fibres extend down and back, joining the posterior collateral ligaments of the pedal joint.

The posterior ligaments of the pastern joint hold the bones together at the rear of the joint.

Ligaments of the pedal joint

The short pastern, pedal and navicular bones are attached to one another to form the coffin joint. The pedal and navicular bones are united by an interosseous ligament and then attached to the short pastern bone by two pairs of collateral ligaments — the anterior and posterior collateral ligaments. The anterior ligaments pass from the side of the short pastern to a depression in the side of the extensor process of the pedal bone. The posterior ligaments are partially a continuation of the anterior fibres of the collateral ligaments of the pastern joint. Each ligament passes down and backwards, with a branch attaching to the wings of the pedal bone and the lateral cartilages. The navicular bone has its own suspensory ligaments which assist in the attachment to the short pastern and pedal bones.

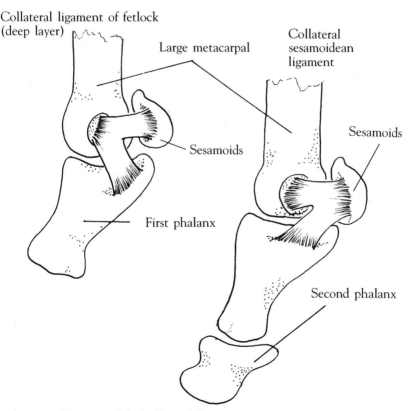

Collateral ligament of fetlock (deep layer)

Large metacarpal

Collateral sesamoidean ligament

Sesamoids

Sesamoids

First phalanx

Second phalanx

Figure 11(a) Collateral ligaments of the lower leg

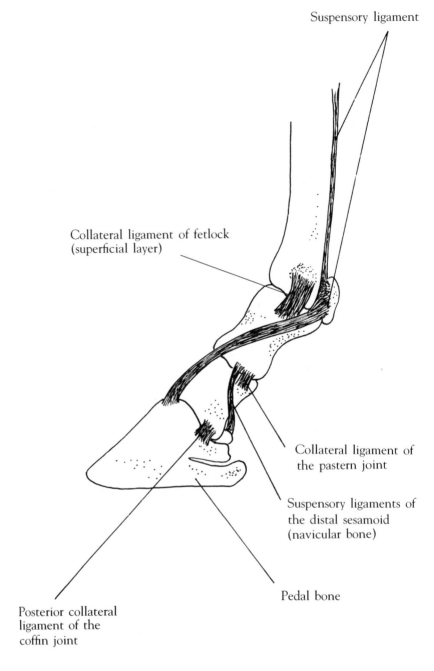

Suspensory ligament

Collateral ligament of fetlock
(superficial layer)

Collateral ligament of
the pastern joint

Suspensory ligaments of
the distal sesamoid
(navicular bone)

Pedal bone

Posterior collateral
ligament of the
coffin joint

Figure 11(b) Collateral ligaments of the lower leg

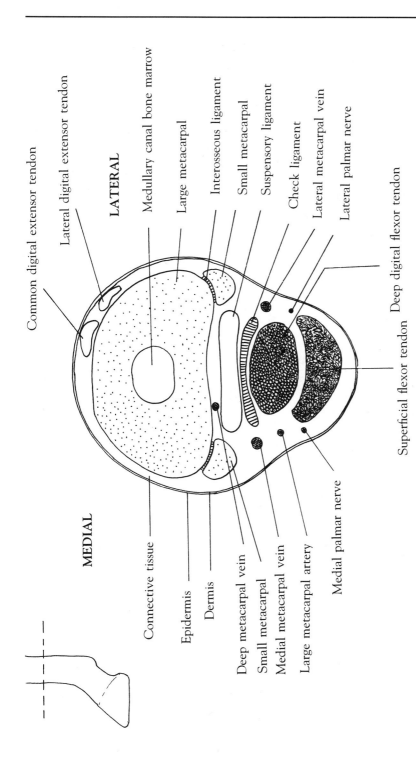

Common digital extensor tendon

Lateral digital extensor tendon

LATERAL

Medullary canal bone marrow

Large metacarpal

Interosseous ligament

Small metacarpal

Suspensory ligament

Check ligament

Lateral metacarpal vein

Lateral palmar nerve

MEDIAL

Connective tissue

Epidermis

Dermis

Deep metacarpal vein

Small metacarpal

Medial metacarpal vein

Large metacarpal artery

Medial palmar nerve

Superficial flexor tendon   Deep digital flexor tendon

Figure 12 Horizontal cross-section through foreleg (midway down large metacarpal)

2

CARE OF THE FEET

The hooves must be picked out at least once a day, preferably twice. If the hoofpick and skip are kept ready to hand, picking out the hooves should become automatic before tacking up, turning out and putting back into the stable. Whilst picking out hooves, look for any signs that the horse may need re-shoeing.

A coat of hoof oil daily keeps the horn looking smart and helps prevent evaporation of moisture. If the horse is prone to brittle hooves, add limestone flour and cod liver oil to the diet to ensure that calcium and vitamins A and D are present in sufficient levels to encourage and promote healthy horn growth.

SHOEING

The main reason for shoeing a horse is to prevent the horny hoof wall from being worn out faster than the rate of growth. Other reasons are:

It enables the horse to work both on and off the roads without excessive wear to the feet, thus preventing footsoreness.

It improves grip on grass and permits the use of studs for competition purposes.

It helps reduce the softening effects of excessive wet and moisture.

It may help correct defects or ailments of the foot.

As a rough guide, the horse will need to be re-shod every six to eight weeks. If the horse is in very hard work or is prone to losing shoes he may need to be shod every five weeks, or even more frequently. It is possible to keep some horses unshod if they are not working particularly hard or are just hacking out on suitable going. However, they will still need to have their feet trimmed every six to eight weeks to ensure even development and balance of the hoof wall.

Signs indicating the need for re-shoeing

A shoe has become worn or loose.

Clenches have risen.

A shoe has been cast (lost).

The foot has grown long and out of shape.

The ends of the shoe are bearing on the sole.

The wall overhangs the shoe.

Six weeks have elapsed since the farrier last attended to the horse.

Preparation for the farrier's visit

Always book appointments with the farrier well in advance. Leaving it until the last minute means you may have a long wait, resulting in a lost shoe or other problems.

Ensure that the horse is well used to being handled and having his feet lifted and picked out.

Someone competent must be on hand to meet the farrier and available to assist if necessary. The horse must be ready — stabled with clean, dry legs. There must be a secure ring to which the horse may be tied.

If possible, provide a level and clean surface for the farrier to work on. In winter, a well lit, sheltered area is essential, preferably with a non-slip floor.

If travelling to the forge, always arrive in time.

The driving hammer is used with the buffer to knock up clenches, and also for knocking in the nails

The buffer is used to knock up the clenches

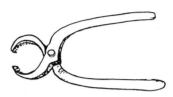

The pincers are used to lever off the shoe. (Hoofcutters look very much like pincers but are sharper and used for cutting the horn)

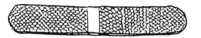

The rasp is used to ensure a level bearing surface, to make beds for the clenches and to finish off the hoof once the shoe is on

The drawing knife is used to pare off ragged pieces of horn from the frog and to shape the bed for the toe clip

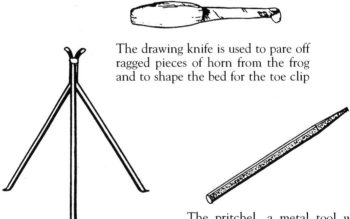

The pritchel, a metal tool with a pointed end, is used to carry the red-hot shoes

The tripod is used to rest the horse's foot upon whilst finishing off with the rasp

Figure 13 The farrier's tools

Handling an unruly horse

Although many horses are nervous by nature, few are aggressive. If a horse is well handled from birth and taught to stand while having his feet attended to, there should be no problems when the farrier visits. However, if a horse is difficult, it must be agreed between the farrier and owner how the horse is to be restrained and/or reprimanded. The farrier will normally use his voice to correct the horse. If vocal reprimands are insufficient, further means of restraint such as a bridle or twitch will need to be implemented. In severe cases it may be necessary, after consultation with the vet, to use sedatives and/or tranquillizers.

Shoeing procedure

Removing the shoe. The horse's foot is held between the farrier's legs. The clenches are knocked up using the buffer and driving hammer. Then, using the pincers, the shoe is levered off, starting at the heels and working down towards the toe.

Preparing the foot. The hoofcutters and/or paring knife will be used to remove excessive horn growth. The bearing surface of the foot will then be levelled off with the rasp. A small nick or 'bed' is made in the wall for the toe or quarter clips.

Forging the shoe. The correct length and weight of iron is cut. The iron is held in the forge until red-hot, then shaped around the anvil. The nail holes are stamped in and finally toe or quarter clips are drawn. The front shoes have toe clips and the hind shoes have quarter clips to help hold the shoe in place. Toe clips are not used behind as this would exacerbate overreaching (the toe of the hind foot striking the heel of the front foot causing bruising or laceration). The toe of the hind shoe may be rounded off (rolled) to reduce any damage done in the event of the horse overreaching.

Many farriers buy in their shoes ready made and, if the hot shoeing process is used, they simply heat the shoe in the furnace and shape it accurately to the shape of the horse's foot.

Fitting the shoe. If the hot shoeing method is used, the shoe is heated as above and held with a pritchel onto the prepared hoof. The burn mark left on the foot gives the farrier an indi-cation as to what alterations need to be made. These are made while the shoe is still very hot. Once the shoe fits absolutely correctly, it is immersed in cold water to cool.

When cold shoeing, the farrier holds the shoe against the foot and will use the hammer and anvil to alter the shape as necessary. However, hot shoeing permits easier alteration of the shoe, so therefore a better fit.

Nailing on. Shoeing nails vary in size and are bevelled on one side. The nails are driven in with the bevel to the inside to send the nail outwards, thus reducing the risk of the nail penetrating the sensitive foot. As each nail is driven in the point is twisted off, leaving just enough to make a clench. The nails are never sent back in the old nail holes, but always go in a slightly different position to ensure a good hold. Seven nails are used; three on the inner edge of the shoe and four on the outer edge.

Finishing off. The farrier encourages the horse to rest one foot forward on the tripod. The farrier then makes a small indentation in the wall just below the nail points. This forms a bed for the clench to lie in. The clenches are hammered over, bedded in and then smoothed over with the rasp. The toe clip is tapped into its bed.

The foot is then rasped lightly to tidy up where foot and shoe meet. Once the whole procedure has been completed, the horse should trot up perfectly sound.

Signs of good shoeing

Every time any horse is shod, there are two fundamental points to be considered — the normal functions of the foot must not be impaired, and the shoes must not detract from the horse's normal action. Individual signs of good shoeing are:

1) The horse must be completely sound and able to move freely and comfortably.

2) The shoe must be made to fit the foot and not vice versa. Excessive cutting back of the toe is known as 'dumping'. There should have been no excessive paring away of the frog or sole. The hoof wall should be trimmed to the best natural shape.

3) The correct weight and thickness of iron must be used according to the size of the horse or pony and the work he is expected to carry out. For example, a riding school cob will have fairly heavy shoes while a 12.2 hh show pony will wear very lightweight shoes.

4) The correct size of nail must be used. The nail holes must be evenly spaced between the toe and the quarter.

5) The nails should emerge one third of the way up the foot, not too low down the wall. The latter is known as 'fine nailing' and presents the risk of the shoe being wrenched off, possibly tearing the hoof wall.

6) The nail heads should fit the nail holes in the shoe so that they are level with the surface of the shoe.

7) The frog should be in contact with the ground.

8) There must be no daylight between the wall and the shoe.

9) The shoe must be long enough to support the heel and ensure no loss of bearing surface of the foot.

10) There should not be excessive rasping away of the periople.

11) All toe and quarter clips should be neatly embedded in the wall.

Types of shoe for normal use

The concave fullered shoe known as the hunter shoe is the most common type in everyday use. It is narrower at the ground surface than at the bearing surface. The ground surface is fullered that is, it has a groove cut into the iron and the inner edge is concave to improve grip.

The heels of the front shoe are pencilled (tapered off) to help prevent the toe of the hind shoe from catching and pulling off the front shoe. To improve grip further, a square-shaped calkin is often added onto the outside heel while the inside heel is fitted with a rounded wedge to balance the foot. (Calkins are not fitted to the inner heel because of the risk of injury). The hind shoes have quarter clips and the front shoes have toe clips.

Plain stamped shoes (with no fullering or concave shaping) may be used on horses and ponies doing slow work.

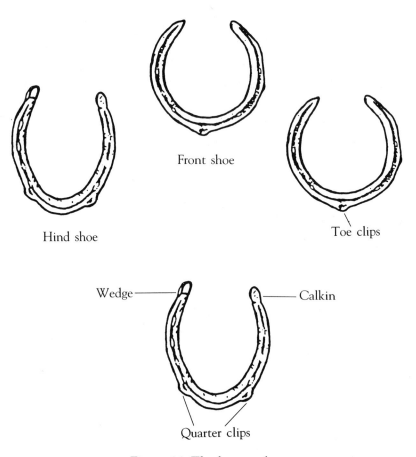

Front shoe

Hind shoe

Toe clips

Wedge —————   ————— Calkin

Quarter clips

Figure 14 The hunter shoe

THE NORMAL FUNCTIONS OF THE FOOT

The foot has evolved specially to perform the following functions:

Bear the horse's weight.

Reduce concussion and promote blood circulation.

Protect sensitive internal structures.

Act as a defence aid when used for kicking and striking out.

In order to understand how the foot performs these functions it is necessary to have a knowledge of what actually happens when the foot comes into contact with the ground. As the foot touches the ground, the weight is transmitted via the bones to the bearing surfaces of the hoof and frog. Because the heel comes to the ground first, the important anti-concussion structures are at the rear of the foot.

Pressure on the frog exerts pressure onto the digital cushion which forces the lateral cartilages apart, against the horny wall. This flattens and empties the blood vessels between the lateral cartilages and the wall. At this stage the heels expand approximately 1.8−2.5 mm ($\frac{1}{15}-\frac{1}{10}$ in) depending upon the size of the animal.

The shape of the hoof will vary slightly according to the different forces exerted upon it. Factors which affect these forces include:

The speed at which the horse is travelling.

The nature of the going underfoot.

The size of the foot in relation to the size of the horse.

Any defects in conformation.

Any defects in the gait.

Once the pressure is relieved when the foot is lifted off the ground, the foot will contract slightly, relaxing the digital cushion, so the blood vessels between the lateral cartilages and the wall will refill.

THE PASTERN AND FOOT AXES

If the functions of the foot are impaired by improper or irregular shoeing, adverse changes may occur. Therefore, a level bearing surface must be provided. To ensure this, the axis lines of the pastern and foot must be checked from both front and side.

Front view. An imaginary vertical line (marked 'X' on Figure 15) should extend down from the centre of the fetlock joint to the centre of the toe, which should point straight forwards. There should be an even amount of foot either side of the line — the two halves should match.

(Viewed from beneath, the bearing surface of the front foot should appear virtually circular. The measurement taken from one heel to the tip of the toe should be the same as the measurement taken across the widest point of the quarters. The hind foot is more oval in shape, being slightly pointed at the toe.)

Figure 15 A normal foot viewed from the front

Side view. When viewed from the side, the imaginary line of the pastern axis starts at the centre of the fetlock joint and runs forwards and downwards through the long and short pastern bones, cutting them in half lengthways. A continuation of that line from the coronet to the bearing surface indicates the foot axis. The foot axis should be at the same angle as the front of the wall — approximately 45–50 degrees in the forelimbs and 50–55 degrees in the hind limbs. (See Figure 16).

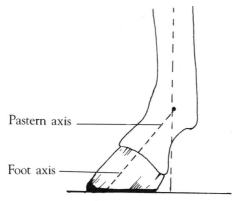

Figure 16 Normal pastern/foot axis

Abnormal pastern and foot axes

Abnormalities of these axes may be natural (a result of conformational defects), or caused by excessive growth of horn at
either the toe or the heel.

Figure 17 shows a foot which has a straight pastern/foot axis
but naturally slopes more than the norm. The angle of the axis
is less than 45 degrees in the forefeet and less than 50 degrees
behind.

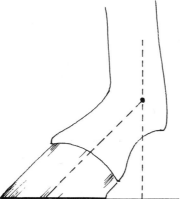

Figure 17 Pastern/foot axis which naturally slopes more than normal

Figure 18 shows an abnormal sloping pastern/foot axis resulting
from excessive horn growth at the toe. The line is broken at
the coronet, indicating that the foot is out of alignment with
the pastern. This can be corrected by reducing the horn at the

toe accordingly. Incorrect alignment which results in excessive sloping of the pastern/foot axis leads to ligament and tendon strain. If allowed to persist, this can have far-reaching effects on the horse's soundness.

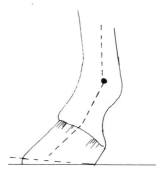

Figure 18 Abnormally sloping pastern/foot axis caused by excessive horn growth

Figure 19 shows a naturally upright pastern/foot axis— the toe is short and the heel high. The angle increases to more than 50 degrees in the forefeet and 55 degrees behind.

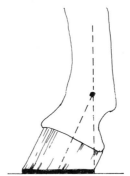

Figure 19 Naturally upright pastern/foot axis

Figure 20 shows the effect on the pastern/foot axis when the horn grows excessively at the heel. Again, the foot axis is out of alignment with the pastern axis, breaking forwards at the coronet. This can be corrected by trimming the heel accordingly. If not corrected, this abnormally upright pastern/foot axis will cause increased jarring of the limb which may lead to concussion-related lameness.

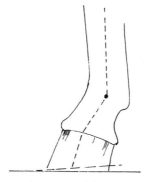

Figure 20 Abnormally upright pastern/foot axis resulting from excessive horn growth

THE HORSE'S ACTION

When assessing the action of a horse, look for straight and level movement. To assess straightness, the horse should be led away from, and back towards, the observer at walk and trot on an even surface. A horse moves straight when the toes point straight forward, the limbs move in alignment with the body and the feet are set down flat. To observe the levelness of the steps the observer must look from the side — each foot should appear to follow a smooth and even arc.

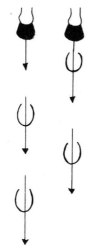

Figure 21 Straight movement

The horse's conformation will have a direct effect upon his way of going and the distribution of bodyweight. Abnormalities of gait may be a result of injury or disease or a consequence of some conformational defect. The latter cannot usually be altered, but the adverse effects can be minimized by correct and expert shoeing. Defects occurring in youngstock can sometimes be corrected by the farrier because the bones are still growing.

Defects of limb conformation which will affect the action include:

Pigeon toes (toe-in). The limbs move in a circular motion; the foot moves outwards then inwards resulting in extra wearing of the outer edge of the wall and exertion of greater pressure on the outer ligaments of the knee. This action is often referred to as 'paddling' or 'dishing'.

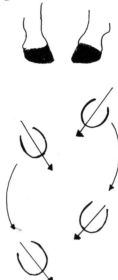

Figure 22 Action as a result of pigeon toes

Splay feet (toe-out). The limbs move inwards then outwards in a circular motion, exerting extra pressure on the inner ligaments and bones of the knee and the inside of the wall becomes worn quickly. Horses with splay feet are prone to brushing. This action is often referred to as 'winging'. Should one leg pass almost in front of the other, this is known as 'plaiting'.

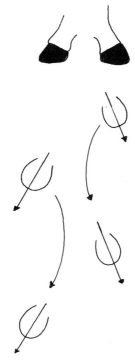

Figure 23 Action as a result of splay feet

Action and wear of the shoes

The wear of a shoe will give a good indication of any faulty action caused by conformation defects; the shoe *should* wear evenly all around. Unevenness of wear may result from one or a combination of the following:

Conformation defect, such as pigeon toes or splay feet.

Abnormality of gait — dishing or plaiting.

Undiagnosed lameness.

Faulty preparation of the foot resulting in an uneven bearing surface.

Pastern/foot axis defect.

Wrong type of shoe used, for example, too heavy.

Common causes of excessive wear to different parts of the shoe, together with corrections, are as follows:

Excessive wear of the toe

Possible causes:

Toe of foot too long.

Excessively high calkins.

Horse adapting action and stance to alleviate pain, as seen in navicular syndrome.

Scraping at floor constantly.

To correct:

Remove cause.

Roll toe of shoe to reduce jarring as toe comes to the ground.

(The farrier would not generally advocate making the shoe thicker at the toe as this would affect the balance of the foot.)

Excessive wear at the quarters

Possible causes:

Pigeon toes or splay-footed conformation.

Uneven bearing surface.

Abnormal pastern/foot axis.

To correct:

Lower one side to match the other and make equal.

When treating pigeon toes the farrier may reduce the edge of the shoe from the inside toe almost back to the quarter. The edge will be rounded off and fitted close. The outer edge, toe to quarter, should be a little wider than normal. When treating splay feet the procedure is reversed.

Excessive wear of the heels

Possible causes:

Chronic laminitis.

Low ringbone.

To correct:

Deal with the cause.

Fit rocker or roller motion shoe, allowing ease of break-over. (Break-over is the term used to describe the point at which the foot is lifted from the ground as the horse takes a step.)

3

CORRECTIVE AND THERAPEUTIC SHOEING

In some cases, the demands made upon a farrier will go beyond ensuring that a sound horse is correctly shod. Possibly in consultation with a vet, a skilled farrier may be able to minimize the effects of certain conditions liable to cause unsoundness and to counteract the consequences of injury or disease. Such specialized shoeing can be summarized thus:

Corrective shoes are generally used to counter defective conformation of the limbs which, in turn, improves the horse's action and thus prevents interferences such as brushing.

Therapeutic shoes are designed to assist in the treatment of lameness caused by disease or injury by offering protection and relieving or exerting pressure as appropriate.

CORRECTIVE SHOEING

The following action defects may be helped by corrective shoeing:

Brushing—the inner edges of the lower leg striking together whilst working.

Speedy-cutting—high brushing.

Overreaching — the toe of the hind shoe strikes the heel of the forefoot whilst working, causing contusions and/or lacerations.

Forging—the toe of the hind shoe catches the inner edge of the corresponding fore shoe toe, causing a loud clicking noise whilst working.

Stumbling—this may vary from a mild stumble to the more serious problem of the horse going right down on his knees.

(A more passive form of interference which is caused by the heel of the front shoe is that leading to capped elbows. This may occur when the horse is lying down in his stable. Treatment usually involves use of a sausage boot to prevent the heel from rubbing the elbow. Bedding must be very deep to prevent the horse going through to the concrete floor when lying down.)

Brushing and speedy-cutting

The initial cause of the brushing should first be established. In some cases, the problem can be alleviated simply by using lighter shoes. If, however, it is caused by faulty limb conformation, this should be dealt with if possible. Any corrections will need to be carried out gradually by the farrier. By countering conformation defects and faulty action the problem of brushing may well be eliminated. The farrier will ensure that the foot is level and balanced.

If, despite efforts to improve the action, the horse is still prone to brushing, he may need to wear anti-brushing shoes. The most common form are known as knocked-up shoes. The inner branch of such a shoe is narrower than the outer and has no nail holes. The ground surface of the inner branch slopes downward and inward and is well rounded off. There may be one or two nail holes at the toe. The outer branch has nail holes and possibly a quarter clip to prevent the shoe from slipping. The inner branch of the shoe is fitted very close to the wall—any overhanging wall is well rasped to ensure a smooth and rounded surface.

A more exaggerated version of the knocked-up shoe is often referred to as a feather-edged shoe. This is sometimes made with the inner edge slightly raised in an attempt to alter the path of the foot as a means of preventing brushing.

Shoes known as anti-speedy cut may be adapted for use with horses who brush and/or speedy-cut. These generally are nearly normal, except that the inner branch is straight and 'blind' (no nail holes) from the toe to the quarter. The outer edge of the inner branch is well rounded and has one or two nail holes at the heel. Once fitted, the overhanging wall is rasped flush.

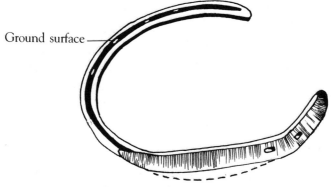

Ground surface

Figure 24 Speedy-cut front shoe

The main disadvantages of working horses in such shoes are:

The difficulty in securing the 'blind' branch—this may lead to the shoe being easily wrenched off.

The reduced bearing surface may lead to uneven weight distribution.

The close fitting of the inner branch may lead to pressure points on the sole.

They do not generally offer good grip.

Any shoe designed to alleviate brushing or speedy-cutting must be carefully made and fitted to suit the problem of the individual horse.

Overreaching and forging

These two interferences require similar shoeing. The object of shoeing to prevent overreaching and forging is to speed up the time taken to move the front foot forwards and off the ground ('break-over time'), to slow down the break-over of the hind foot and to lessen the risk of damage should the horse strike himself with the toe of the hind shoe.

The front shoes may have the heels slightly raised and the toes rolled. The heels may be shortened and well bevelled to prevent the hind toe from catching them. The hind shoe will be set back at the toe and any overhanging wall rasped flush to the shoe. To delay the break-over, the heels of the shoe are lowered slightly and left long which has a 'dragging' (slowing) effect. The toe of the hind shoe may be squared off, sometimes referred to as a 'club toe'. The front edge of the toe is well rounded as it slopes towards the ground surface. (This is not the same thing as 'dumping', which is simply an attempt to make a wrong-sized shoe fit.)

Ground surface

Figure 25 Overreach shoe

Stumbling

This may be caused by the horse catching his toe on the ground for one or more of the following reasons:

Tiredness and/or unfitness (muscle weakness).

Lameness.

Reduced flexion of the fetlock joint, for example as a result of arthritic changes.

Overgrown toes.

The ground surface edge too square on a newly shod foot.

As with all faults of action, the primary cause must be dealt with first, then consideration given to the aspect of corrective shoeing.

The shoe needs to be shaped to prevent the toe from coming into contact with the ground too early and 'digging in'. This may be achieved by rasping the toe fairly short and 'rolling' or 'setting up' the toe. The toe is rolled by setting up the front half of the bearing surface at the toe at an angle of approximately 25 degrees. The heels may be raised slightly to minimize any 'dragging' effect.

THERAPEUTIC SHOEING

Lameness as a result of injury or disease may be alleviated through the selective use of special therapeutic shoes. The farrier and vet will advise as to what shoes are needed and, indeed, each individual horse will require 'made-to-measure' therapeutic shoes. The farrier may adapt the well known types of therapeutic shoe (see Figure 26) to suit the needs of the horse.

Types of therapeutic shoe

The many different patterns of therapeutic shoe can be categorized according to their purpose.

Shoes to aid distribution of pressure on the base of the foot

Seated out shoe. The bearing surface is reduced to relieve pressure on the sole, therefore the seated out shoe may be used for any condition where pressure needs to be relieved from the sole, for example corns, dropped or bruised sole. Disadvantages of this shoe are that the seated out area tends to fill with debris and, in deep going, the shoe is easily pulled off.

Three-quarter shoe. This shoe, which has half of one branch missing, has been used on horses suffering from corns. The main disadvantage of this shoe is the lack of protection afforded to the bruised area and the lack of support, resulting in the uneven distribution of weight. For these reasons, the three-quarter shoe is not in popular use.

T-bar shoe. Shaped like an anchor, this shoe consists of a tip connected to a plate which extends back and covers the frog. This, also, has been used for corns but, while it transfers pressure onto the frog, it does not protect the bruised areas. At one time it was used to treat contracted heels. However, it is prone to being ripped off, so is not very practical and is not nowadays in general use.

Bar shoe. A bar, upon which the frog sits, is welded onto the heels of the shoe. This transfers weight from the heels onto the frog. It is therefore useful in conditions which require increased frog pressure and/or decreased pressure on the heels.

Heart-bar shoe. So named because of its shape, this shoe is currently very popular because of its effectiveness in the treatment of laminitis. It has a V-shaped bar welded to the heels of the shoe, upon which the frog sits. This offers support to the pedal bone, thus helping to reduce the risk of pedal bone rotation and also gives increased frog pressure, which helps to improve circulation within the foot.

Egg-bar shoe. A rounded bar extends back beyond the heels, giving the shoe an egg-shaped outline. It is used in the treatment of navicular syndrome and weakened heels.

Three-quarter bar shoe. This shoe is sometimes used when treating a single corn. It has a bar welded onto one heel, but the heel on the affected side has approximately 2.5−4 cm (1−1½ in) removed. This shoe supports the heels and takes pressure off the seat of the corn, although the bruised area has no protection.

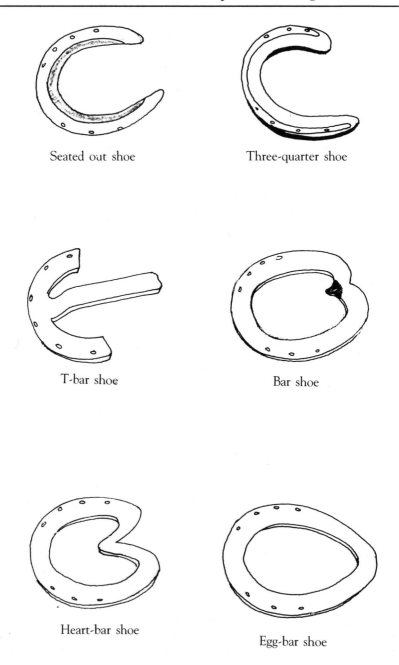

Seated out shoe

Three-quarter shoe

T-bar shoe

Bar shoe

Heart-bar shoe

Egg-bar shoe

Figure 26 Therapeutic shoes

Three-quarter bar shoe

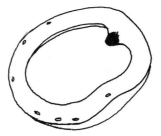

Rocker-bar shoe

Patten shoe

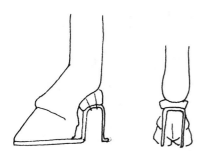

Swan-necked shoe

Rocker-bar shoe. As with the other bar shoes, this gives increased frog pressure. The shape of the shoe helps to minimize concussion and assists in promoting a more normal action as the foot comes to the ground. The web of the shoe (the width and thickness of the metal), is twice that of a normal shoe at the quarters. It gets thinner towards the heels and the toes, so giving a 'rocker' effect when the foot comes into contact with the ground. It has been used in conditions such as laminitis; as the affected animal puts his heel to the ground, the shape of the shoe leads the foot to 'roll' onto the toe. It is also useful in the relief of ringbone and arthritic conditions. It is, however, only of use at slow paces.

Shoes to relieve pressure on tendons and joints

There are many conditions which benefit from having the heels raised to relieve pressure on tendons and joints. The main disadvantage of raising the heels of a shoe is the loss of frog pressure which follows. However, this can be avoided if a rubber wedge-shaped pad is used between the foot and the shoe. This raises the heels, maintains frog pressure and has anti-concussive qualities.

Whenever the heels of a shoe are raised, it is important that the toe is well rolled to lessen the risk of 'digging in' and to improve the mobility of the limb.

Patten shoe. This has a raised bar, which rests on the ground, welded to the heels of the shoe. The height of the bar will range from 2.5–7.5 cm (1–3 in) dependent upon the size of the horse and the severity of the injury. This shoe is useful when treating deep digital flexor tendon injuries and navicular syndrome.

Swan-necked shoe. The heels of this shoe continue upwards to the lower aspect of the rear of the fetlock joint, curve over and extend downwards back to the ground. A padded 'bridge', upon which the fetlock joint is supported, is welded onto these two extensions.

This drastic form of shoeing may be needed when dealing

with ruptured flexor tendons and/or suspensory ligaments. The padded support of the shoe would need to be very carefully and gradually lowered under the supervision of both farrier and vet to avoid permanent contraction of the tendons.

Glue-on shoes

In recent years, great progress has been made in the design and feasibility of plastic glue-on shoes. There are occasions when the wall of the foot is too cracked and weak to nail a shoe onto. In cases of severe lameness, nailing-on can cause great pain. The glue-on shoes are generally made of polyurethane and have finger-like projections by which the shoe is glued to the hoof wall.

Some shoes have an aluminium inner core, bonded in 100 per cent polyurethane for added wear, strength and shock absorption. This type can be hammered on the anvil to gain an accurate fit and has been used with success on racehorses.

One form of plastic shoe, known as the 'Glue II', is shaped from a solid pad of polyurethane. The foot is x-rayed and the shoe shaped individually. The 'Glue II' can also be adapted to form heart-bar shoes, used in the treatment of laminitis. Specially designed glue-on shoes can be shaped for therapeutic purposes and used in the early corrective treatment of foals. Examples of such treatment are lateral extensions for foals with angular limb deformities and toe extensions for foals with contracted tendons.

When glue-on shoes are fitted, the hoof wall is lightly rasped and sanded to provide a smooth, clean, gluing surface. The shoe adheres more securely to the foot when less glue is used — it also sets more quickly, reducing the risk of the shoe slipping. The shoes should fit as snugly as possible to help reduce slipping.

The shoes generally stay on for four to six weeks and may be used for road work and in the winter. When the shoes have to be removed, the tabs are loosened off by running a knife between the shoe and the wall.

4

LAMENESS

Lameness is a disturbance of the horse's natural gait, normally caused by pain and is a sign that disease or injury is present. Examination of the horse is necessary to find out which leg he is lame on and the nature of the disease or injury.

It is necessary to be able to differentiate between lameness, as caused by disease or injury and a defective gait, as caused by faulty conformation or stiffness arising from age or fatigue.

EXAMINATION TO DIAGNOSE LAMENESS

The initial examination may be divided into the following procedures:

Reference to medical history and reported signs.

Observation at rest.

Observation during movement.

Palpation of the limbs.

Passive movement of the joints.

Examination may reveal the cause of lameness — if not it will at least provide information for the vet.

If, after the above procedures have been followed, the cause of the lameness has not become apparent, the veterinary surgeon will employ more sophisticated measures, such as nerve blocking and x-ray, to detect the problem. Let us examine these diagnostic procedures in more detail:

Medical history and reported signs

The first point to consider is whether there is a relevant history of illness or lameness. Also, has the horse recently slipped badly or fallen whilst jumping/working, or been kicked or cast in his box? Other background points to note are:

Breeding and age.

The purpose for which he is kept. If for competition, the type of competition and details of performance at these events.

Whether the horse is stabled, grass-kept or a combination of both.

Diet. Any vitamin or mineral supplements must be noted. Also, does he have a healthy appetite?

When the horse has been ridden, have there been signs of:

Stiffness, resistance or evasion of the bit?

A 'cold back' or excessive hollowing?

Difficulty when going either up or downhill?

An unwillingness to jump?

A frequent change of leg at canter or gallop?

The horse trying to 'bump' the rider from one diagonal to another at rising trot?

Other pertinent questions are:

When did the horse become lame/for how long has he been lame?

Was the onset of lameness sudden and, if so, what was the horse doing at the time?

Are there any swellings, soft or hard, that are normal or abnormal on the horse's limbs?

Have any new signs of heat or swelling arisen since the lameness?

Once all these facts have been established, the observation can begin.

Observation at rest

Without entering the stable, observe the horse's general stance:

Does he stand with the weight distributed evenly on all four legs? Resting a hind leg is no cause for concern, but resting or 'pointing' a foreleg is usually indicative of trouble.

Does he shift his weight from one forefoot to another? This may be seen if pain is present in both forefeet, for example with laminitis. Also, does the horse lie down excessively?

Has he dug up his bedding? Horses with pain in the heel region of the foot may stand with their heels raised on mounds of bedding.

Note the overall condition as best you can bearing in mind he may still be rugged up — does the horse look disinterested or in pain?

Having put on the headcollar, try to position the horse so that he is on a level surface, preferably not a bedded-down floor. Good light is essential if you are to examine the horse properly.

Pick up the feet; pick out and examine. Feel for heat in the hoof wall.

Look at the pastern/foot axis of all four limbs — are the respective pairs similar?

Look at the size and shape of the feet—are the respective pairs the same?

Remove any rugs and note temperature, pulse and respiration rates—any increases in rate may indicate pain and/or infection. (NB: the horse's normal resting rates must be known for this to be of value.)

Look at the muscular development on each side—it should be even. Note any lumps or sores on the spine. Look at the horse from behind—the hips should appear level.

Once you have made these observations you will need to see the horse in movement. The exceptions to this would be in the case of obvious tendon/ligament breakdown or if a fracture is suspected.

Observation during movement

First note the wear of the shoes, if shod.

A hard and level surface is needed. Depending upon the degree of lameness, it may be apparent at walk. If the lameness is of a mild nature it is preferable to move the horse into trot straight away before the lameness 'walks off'. A steady trot on a loose rein will show up most types of lameness. However, if the horse is trotted too quickly this may actually disguise a problem. As well as being led on a straight line the horse should be lunged on a hard surface, as this often accentuates the effects of unsoundness.

In addition to *looking* for lameness you can also *listen* for any irregularities in the hoof beats, although it is necessary for the horse to be either shod or unshod all round in order to hear a clear beat.

Foreleg lameness

When the problem is in one limb only, the withers, neck and head appear to lower as the sound leg comes to the ground. As the unsound leg bears the weight, the horse raises his head—this hoof beat may also sound lighter.

If the horse is lame in both front limbs, the steps will be short and pottery and the action stilted, with decreased shoulder movement. If the lameness is fairly equal in each limb there may be no nodding of the head and the horse may appear to be 'going even'.

If one leg is worse than the other a degree of head nodding is generally visible — but the less lame leg must not be overlooked. Nerve blocking of the worse leg will show up the lameness in the other limb more noticeably.

Hind leg lameness

As the lame hind leg comes to the ground, the croup will be raised and the step made lighter. The result of raising the croup is that the head and neck will be lowered. As the sound hind leg comes to the ground, so this is reversed — the croup lowers and the head and neck are raised.

If both hind legs are unsound, the stride will be shortened and the action wobbly and/or straddling in manner. The horse may also find it difficult to step backwards.

Watching the horse move from the side enables any variations in length of stride or reduced flexion of joints to be observed. When the horse is turned, notice how he bears weight on the inside hind leg. Turning the horse tightly around on the spot may accentuate the effects of a hind leg problem.

Palpation of the limbs

The suspect limb must now be examined carefully for signs of heat, swelling and/or pain.

The foot should be picked out again and, if muddy, scrubbed. Ninety per cent of all lamenesses originate in the foot. It is therefore imperative that the foot is carefully examined first. A drawing knife should be used to scrape at the sole, allowing you to check the sole for bruising or possible puncture wounds. Assess the condition of the shoe, making a note of any uneven wear. Feel the walls of each pair of hooves and compare. Hoof testers may be used to apply pressure around the hoof. The horse will be likely to flinch if pain is felt. Any sole pads will have to be removed before the hoof tester is used. If lameness within the foot is suspected, it may be necessary to have the shoe removed and to look further for bruising, corns, puncture wounds or an abscess.

If the cause of any foot lameness is still not apparent the advice of the vet must be sought, as x-rays will be necessary in order to determine which area within the foot is affected.

Assuming that the problem does not appear to be within the foot, continue the examination of the limb by feeling around the coronary band and heels. It is in this area, to the rear of the foot, that sidebones may be felt. Instead of being able to compress the coronet, a hard, bony lump may be felt. Also, feel the front of the pastern — a lump here could indicate the formation of a high ringbone.

Next, continue to work up the pastern to the fetlock joint. Heat and swelling laterally may indicate damage to one or more of the ligaments of the joint, whilst inflammation at the rear of the joint could indicate sesamoiditis.

Between the fetlock joint and the knee or hock, a careful examination must be made of the ligaments and tendons. Swellings are not always the result of strain — the swelling may 'pit' upon the application of pressure, and may be caused by an infection. 'Pitting' indicates oedema or tissue fluid accumulation — this may be seen in any inflammatory condition, whether infectious or not. However, joint infections are not usually accompanied by oedema in the acute phase.

Swelling may also be found on the inside of the limb, in the region of the splint bones.

In the foreleg the knee, elbow and shoulder must be examined and, in the hind leg, the hock, stifle and hip.

At all the above stages, compare the suspect limb to the sound one.

Passive movement of the joints

In what is usually referred to as a flexion test, the individual joint* is flexed manually to stress the ligaments and so

* Note that it is not possible to flex the hock without the stifle and vice versa.

accentuate any problems. The joint is flexed to the limit of its range and held in this position for approximately one to two minutes. The horse is then trotted on and any increase of lameness noted. This test can be adapted for most of the joints of the limbs:

When trying to identify lameness in the shoulder, the foreleg should be extended as far forward as possible. The horse may well indicate pain by pulling backwards violently.

Stifle lameness may be shown by the horse keeping the stifle joint mostly flexed whether at rest or during movement.

A problem in the hip may cause the toe to move outward instead of in straight alignment with the body. If pain is felt in the joints of the hind limb, the horse will seem to hold his leg up and keep weight off it whilst the flexion test is being carried out.

The joints may be extended, as opposed to flexed, by standing the horse on a wedge (toe up) for one to two minutes. Trotting on immediately may show up a more marked lameness in some instances.

Checking the spine

If it is suspected that the problem lies within the spine, it is possible to check whether the horse has a normal range of spinal movement. This is best done before exercise, to ensure the muscles have not loosened up. The range of movement is as follows:

Ventroflexion (arching).

Dorsiflexion (hollowing).

Lateral (side) flexion.

To test for ventroflexion, press a hand firmly beneath the abdomen just behind the girth line — this should result in the horse arching his spine.

The horse should hollow away from pressure applied either

side of the withers, and running a hand firmly down the length of his back applying pressure either side of the spinal process should cause the horse to curve his body away in side flexion. The horse should be capable of turning his neck so that he can touch his ribs with his muzzle on either side.

Any muscular problems affecting the spine must be dealt with by a trained physiotherapist and veterinary surgeon. Check the spine for swellings, saddle sores etc.

Diagnostic aids

In addition to the examination procedure described, the vet may use certain techniques to assist or confirm diagnosis.

Nerve blocking

The vet may block the nerves supplying the suspected area as an aid to a more accurate diagnosis. Local anaesthetic is injected into the area around the nerve, normally starting low down the limb. The effect of the block is checked by assessing skin sensation in the area supplied by the nerve. Once the area is desensitized, the horse is trotted on. If the horse still appears lame, further anaesthetic may be injected around more proximal nerves. Once this has taken effect the horse may be trotted on and, if he is sound, it may be deduced that the problem lies within that particular area.

Radiography (x-ray)

Radiography provides a very reliable method of obtaining a realistic diagnosis, particularly with bone-related problems such as fractures, exostosis (new bone growth), arthritis and decreases in bone density.

There is a wide variety of x-ray machines in use, which transform the electric current from the mains into one of high voltage (measured in kilovolts) but low amperage (measured in milliamps). When this new current passes through an x-ray tube, x-rays are produced. These x-rays travel in straight lines and form what is known as the primary beam, which is directed through the relevant part of the patient. An x-ray machine can be adjusted to alter the x-rays' ability to penetrate; the vet controls the kilovoltage, milliamperage and time of exposure according to the nature of the area to be x-rayed.

Portions of the primary beam will be obstructed or absorbed by the denser structures — this results in the beam casting 'shadows' of the penetrated structures on the x-ray film. Once the x-ray has been taken, the film must be carefully processed by passing through certain chemical solutions, which will then show up the shadow picture.

If an area is not likely to produce distinct shadows, it may be necessary for the vet to introduce a contrast agent into the area in order to show a more positive outline. The contrast agent, opaque to x-rays, is injected prior to taking the x-ray. The resultant image is then known as a reticulogram or mylogram.

It may be necessary to take an x-ray of the corresponding part of the sound limb in order to make a comparison. The combination of clinical observation and the results of radiography should enable an accurate diagnosis to be made.

Examination per rectum

This may prove useful in the diagnosis of diseases which may affect the pelvic and abdominal cavities, thus causing lameness.

5

CAUSES OF LAMENESS

While many causes of lameness are specific to a certain part of the limb, others are essentially generic in nature — they are ailments of the same *type*, given individual names to identify their precise form and location. This is especially true of the various bursal and bony enlargements, and we will discuss these first, before moving on to the more specific ailments.

BURSAL ENLARGEMENTS

The joints of the limbs are free-moving, encased in a fibrous capsule and lubricated by synovial fluid (synovial joints). In order to appreciate the problems which affect these joints, it is necessary to have a basic understanding of the structure of a synovial joint.

In such a joint, the ends of the bones are covered in cartilage which, aided by synovial fluid, reduces friction. This cartilage is very tough and slightly compressible, making it strong enough to withstand great forces. Young cartilage is white and glistening but, with age, becomes yellow and more brittle. It is nourished by the synovial fluid, which is an opaque, pale yellow fluid secreted by the synovial membrane. This membrane lines the non-articular parts of the synovial joint and all tendon sheaths.

The functions of synovial fluid are:

To lubricate a joint and reduce friction within it.

To prevent erosion of the joint surfaces.

To provide nutriment for the articular cartilages. (If a synovial joints has two articular surfaces, it is referred to as a simple joint. If it has more than two surfaces it is known as a compound joint.)

The whole of a joint is encased in a capsular ligament forming a fibrous sac. Through wear, tear and strain the sac sometimes becomes distended, forming a soft, fluid-filled swelling. These swellings are classified as bursal enlargements. (See also Ailments of the Joints – Synovitis and Bursitis.)

A bursa is a closed sac lined by smooth cells (resembling the synovial membrane) which secrete a lubricating fluid. Bursa are positioned between structures where unusual pressure is likely to occur:

1) Between a tendon or muscle and bony prominence.

2) Between fascia and harder tissue.

3) Between skin and underlying fascia joints.

Their functions are to allow free movement between the structures and to reduce strain, tearing and friction.

There are two types of bursa – those which develop before birth and are located in a constant position, and those which are acquired and develop over bony prominences such as the elbow (capped elbow). In many cases, such bursal enlargements do not cause lameness and are best left alone. It must be understood that a horse with bursal enlargements has been subjected to a degree of 'wear and tear', but may be perfectly sound and fit for work. If purchasing a horse with a view to competitive jumping, any swellings should be carefully investigated as they may be indicative of arthritic changes occurring within the joint. The only classes in which the horse may be marked down on the swellings are showing classes, where clean limbs are a prerequisite.

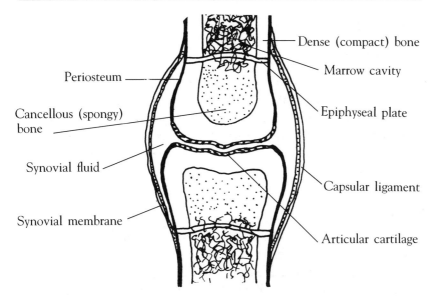

Periosteum

Cancellous (spongy) bone

Synovial fluid

Synovial membrane

Dense (compact) bone

Marrow cavity

Epiphyseal plate

Capsular ligament

Articular cartilage

Figure 27 Structure of a simple synovial joint

Signs, causes and treatment of bursal enlargements

Signs
Heat, pain and swelling whilst forming. There may be some lameness to begin with. Once formed, these swellings are cold and normally do not cause any problems.

Causes
Concussion, for example from excessive trotting or jumping on hard going.
Strain, for example from jumping out of deep mud or pulling up very suddenly in deep going.
Injury, such as a blow, or friction.

Treatment
While forming, cold hosing, hot and cold fomentations and poulticing may help to ease any pain. Massage with embrocation. Generally speaking, bursal enlargements are best left alone, but seek specialist advice about the use of ultrasound, magnetic field therapy or similar. If they are causing lameness, consult the vet.

Types of bursal enlargement

Windgalls

A windgall is a distension of a joint capsule, tendon sheath or bursa with synovial fluid. The term most commonly refers to enlargement of the digital flexor tendon sheath and wind-galls normally form on one or both sides of the fetlock joint, being more common on the hind legs. They are not associated with lameness.

Curb

Found on the back of the hind leg, approximately 10 cm (4 in) below the point of hock. Curbs develop as a result of spraining the plantar tarsal ligament passing over the point of hock. This swelling may become more fibrous with time. A *false curb* is a large head on the metatarsal (splint) bone, showing on the outside of the hock.

Thoroughpin

This results from inflammation of the tendon sheath enclosing the deep flexor tendon. The swelling is seen on the inner and outer side of the hock. This swelling can often be pushed through the hock, which is why it is so named.

Bog spavin

This is an enlargement of the tibiotarsal joint capsule. Swelling is found on the front inner aspect of the hock. Causes include poor conformation, trauma, dietary deficiency and OCD (see Ailments of the Joints).

Capped knee

(Sometimes called hygroma). The front of the knee is enlarged as a result of banging on the stable door or hitting fences. This condition is, therefore, an acquired bursitis resulting from trauma. Although unsightly, a capped knee rarely affects the horse's action.

Capped elbow/hock

These injuries start off as bursal enlargements, but gradually the bursa or joint capsule in the affected area becomes thickened (acquired bursitis.) They are caused by rubbing when the horse is lying down on thin bedding. Sometimes the elbow is capped when the horse lies down and the elbow rests on the shoe of a forefoot. Massage with an embrocation may help alleviate the effects but, once formed, there is very little to be done. If the elbow becomes sore, a sausage boot can be fitted around the pastern, to help stop the heel rubbing. Make sure that the horse always has a good, thick bed.

BONY ENLARGEMENTS

These occur on the different bones of the limb and usually form a hard, bony enlargement.

Signs, causes and treatment of bony enlargements

Signs
Heat, pain and swelling whilst forming, perhaps also some lameness. Often the horse will be sound once the lump is formed, provided that it does not interfere with a joint or tendon.

Causes
Often concussive in origin, for example a result of trotting continually on hard roads, or jumping on very hard ground. Sometimes a kick or blow to the area will lead to a bony enlargement.
Working very young horses too hard, too soon.

Treatment
While bony enlargements are forming, the horse must rest — he can be turned out to grass, but only in a *small* paddock. The heat, pain and swelling can be eased by the following methods, subject to consultation with vet or farrier as appropriate:

Anti-inflammatory injection or powders administered by the vet. Alternatively, the vet may prescribe an anti-inflammatory solution to be rubbed directly onto the affected area.

Cold hosing, cold poultices and ice packs.

Hot and cold fomentations.

The vet may recommend that the enlargement would gain relief from treatment such as Electrovet, laser or ultrasound.

The farrier may fit therapeutic shoes to ease pressure on joints (for example, a horse with bone spavin would benefit from raised heels and rolled toes), or to reduce concussion (a horse with splints would benefit if anti-concussion pads were fitted between the shoe and the foot).

Types of bony enlargement

Ringbone

Ringbone can be either high or low. High ringbone is new bone formation on the distal (lower) end of the long pastern or on the proximal (upper) end of of the short pastern. Low ringbone is new bone formation on the distal end of the short pastern or the proximal aspect of the pedal bone, especially at the extensor process. Low ringbone will have to be confirmed by x-ray.

Sidebones

These bony lumps form as the lateral cartilages ossify (turn to bone). The lateral cartilages extend backwards from either side of the pedal bone. Normally they feel springy when the area above the coronet, towards the heel, is pressed. However, when sidebones are present, this area feels rigid. Sidebones are mainly caused by concussion and the advice of the vet and farrier should be sought.

Splints

These usually form on the inside of the foreleg approximately

6–7 cm below the knee as a result of sprain of the interosseus ligament. They are often seen in young horses whose bones are still developing and who are subjected to undue stress and concussion. Once formed, they are not normally a problem unless a tendon or ligament rubs on the lump, or there is interference with a joint.

Bone spavin

This is arthritis (degeneration) of the distal tarsal joints, with new bone formation. The enlargement may be seen on the front lower part of the inside of the hock. It is a 'wear and tear' condition, accentuated by poor conformation (sickle and cow hocks). Lameness will be accentuated after the hock has been flexion tested. Therapeutic shoeing (raised heel and rolled toe) may be recommended by the farrier. However, despite numerous treatment processes, approximately half of affected horses remain lame and unusable.

AILMENTS OF THE EXTERNAL STRUCTURES OF THE FOOT

Sand crack

Signs
A crack, which can vary from a hairline split to a deep shaft, runs vertically down the wall. If very bad, it will cause lameness.

Causes
Overdrying of the hoof in hot, dry weather.
Excessive rasping of the periople.
Shavings used as bedding material can dry out the hoof wall.
General poor hoof condition caused by lack of vitamins and minerals in the diet.
Lack of trimming.
Injury to the coronet, producing a weak, deformed hoof wall.

Treatment

Consult the farrier, who may stop the crack from becoming worse by making a horizontal groove across the top. He may shoe with clips on either side of the crack to support the wall and repair with the epoxy substance, Technovit. If the crack is severe, it may be infected. The vet may be needed to administer antibiotics. Animalintex poultices will help draw out any infection. Rub a hoof dressing into the coronet; this will encourage healthy horn growth. Adding supplements of biotin, methionine, limestone flour and cod liver oil to the feeds will provide the nutrients which are necessary for healthy hoof growth.

Seedy toe

Signs

The horn becomes brittle and crumbly, leaving a gap at the toe between the wall of the hoof and laminae. The horse may be lame if the condition is severe.

Causes

Concussion of the toe area.

Pressure from the toe clip following an infection after a sand crack.

Diseased laminae (the condition usually accompanies chronic laminitis).

Alternate excessive dampness and dryness.

Treatment

The vet will clean out the cavity and pack with a substance such as hessian covered in Stockholm tar or a hard wax. New hoof growth should be promoted by applying hoof dressing at the coronet. There are many products available; ask the farrier's advice when choosing one. Have the horse shod in such a way as to avoid pressure to the affected area.

Split hoof

Signs

The lower edge of the hoof cracks and breaks away; shoes often fall off easily.

Causes
Failure to have the feet attended to regularly.
Dietary deficiency.
Excessive drying out of the hooves.
Possibly a result of excessive rasping of the periople.

Treatment
Ensure regular and more frequent farriery care and a balanced diet. Add limestone flour and cod liver oil to the diet. There are many feed additives containing biotin (part of the vitamin B complex) which is necessary for good hoof growth — these vary tremendously in price. Limestone flour is relatively inexpensive and provides extra calcium. External preparations are available and are claimed to work well.

Contracted heels

Signs
The heels of the foot become very narrow and contracted.

Causes
Drying out of the wall caused by removal of periople by excessive rasping.
Lack of frog pressure, resulting in poor circulation.

Treatment
A wide-webbed bar shoe (one with a large bearing surface), may be used to encourage the heels to spread and to promote frog pressure.

Thrush

Signs
Foul smell from the clefts of the frog. In severe cases, a black discharge will be present. If left unattended it may result in lameness as the frog becomes eroded and the underlying laminae damaged.

Causes
Bad stable management — failure to pick out the feet daily

combined with the horse standing in dirty/wet bedding, leading to a bacterial infection.

Treatment
Pick out and attend to the feet twice daily without fail, practice good stable management and ensure the horse stands on clean, dry bedding. Pack the clefts of the frog with Stockholm tar (which has antiseptic qualities) or, once the clefts are clean, spray liberally with an antiseptic spray.

The following injuries to the sole of the foot are susceptible to invasion by tetanus bacteria. Therefore, whenever a horse suffers such an injury, it must be a priority to check that tetanus vaccinations are up to date.

Bruised sole

Signs

Lameness, black/red/blue mark on the sole. Pain when pressure is applied by the hoof tester will cause the horse to flinch.

Cause
Stepping on a sharp stone. Horses with flat soles are very prone to bruised soles.

Treatment
Rest on a non-heating diet. Poultice, changed twice daily, will draw out the bruising. Antibiotics may be needed to fight infection. In a severe case, the farrier may cut out the bruise and fit a leather pad between shoe and foot.

Prevention
Have horse shod regularly. Never ride over very stony areas. Pick out feet twice daily to ensure that stones do not become wedged.

Corns

Signs
Bruising appears between the bar and the wall (known as the

'seat of corn'). In severe cases the sensitive laminae will also be bruised, which will cause great pain and lameness. Infection may be present.

Causes

Ill-fitting shoes or shoes left on too long resulting in pressure on the seat of corn. Alternatively, a stone may have become wedged in the shoe.

Treatment

Call either the vet or farrier to remove the shoe and relieve the pressure. They may pare away a small part of the bruised area. If the corn is infected, poulticing will be necessary to draw out the pus. Healing must occur from the inside out to prevent infection being trapped within the sole. A seated out shoe, leaving the area of the corn free, will relieve pressure on the corn, or the farrier may choose to use a leather pad between the shoe and the foot to offer full protection.

Punctured sole

Signs

Lameness occurs as a result of the horse standing on a sharp object such as a nail. If this goes undetected for any length of time there will almost invariably be infection within the foot. Infection involving the important structures of the foot (pedal bone, navicular bursa) may result in permanent unsoundness. Puncture wounds of the middle third of the frog are the most serious as the navicular bursa may be directly damaged. Re-member the precise site of any puncture wound and tell the vet.

Treatment

This will depend on whether or not the nail is still in the foot. If it is, try to prevent the horse from moving around and pushing the nail in further.

You will need: a bowl of water; disinfectant; very hot water in a kettle; Animalintex poultice; two old elasticated bandages; a piece of polythene sheeting; gamgee and either a hoof boot or a large square of hessian sacking.

Scrub the foot and carefully remove the nail. If bleeding occurs do not panic — it will bring out any dirt that has entered the foot. Soak the ready-cut square of Animalintex in nearly boiling water. Wring out the excess water and place the impregnated side of the poultice to the sole of the foot. Press in place firmly and cover with a piece of polythene, then a large square of gamgee. Completely bandage the whole foot with one of the old elasticated bandages. Then bandage the lower limb with a stable bandage and padding such as gamgee. This supports the limb and evens out pressure. Next, either put on the hoof boot or, if using hessian sacking, place the horse's foot in the centre of the square, draw up the corners and bandage firmly in place. The sacking offers protection to the poulticed foot (see Figure 28.) Bandage the sound leg with a normal stable bandage as this will give extra support and prevent filling.

If the nail is no longer in the foot, it will be necessary to find the point of penetration by scrubbing the foot. Heat in the foot will indicate infection. Call the vet to administer antibiotics to reduce the infection and to give a tetanus antitoxin injection if there is any doubt as to whether vaccinations are up to date. The vet may open the hole and pare away a little of the sole to allow the escape of pus. The next stage is to poultice the foot in the method described above. Poultices should be changed twice daily or as instructed by the vet. Once the infection has been completely drawn out, the hole can be plugged with a small piece of cotton wool to prevent dirt from entering the foot.

Key points to remember with puncture wounds

1) Because of the risk of damage to internal structures, puncture wounds can be very serious, with the possibility of permanent damage.
2) The horse must be up to date with his tetanus inoculations.
3) The wound must heal from the inside out to prevent infection developing within the foot.
4) The foot must be kept scrupulously clean to prevent dirt from entering the foot.
5) The farrier may have to shoe using a leather pad to give protection to the damaged area.

(1)   Scrub the foot

(2)

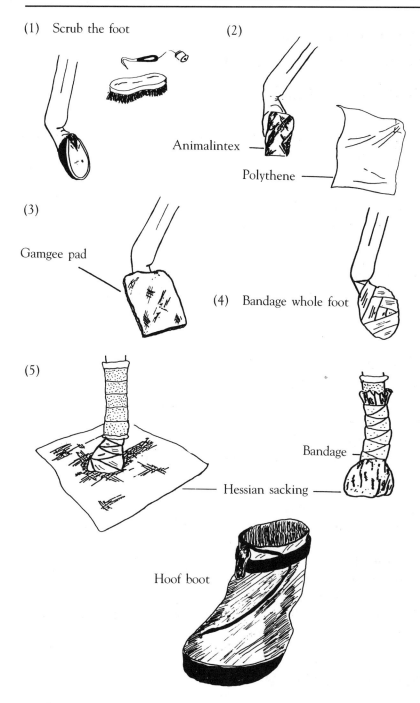

Animalintex

Polythene

(3)

Gamgee pad

(4)   Bandage whole foot

(5)

Bandage

Hessian sacking

Hoof boot

Figure 28 Applying a poultice to a puncture wound of the foot

AILMENTS OF THE INTERNAL STRUCTURES OF THE FOOT

Nail prick and nail bind

Signs
Acute lameness upon having a new shoe put on. Possibly heat in the affected foot.

Causes
The farrier nails too close to the white line and either penet-rates the sensitive laminae (nail prick) or causes great pressure (nail bind).

Treatment
Removal of the nail should bring immediate relief unless there is a complication with infection.

Quittor

Signs
An abscess forms within the lateral cartilages and bursts above the coronary band. While the abscess is forming there will be heat and pain in the foot and the horse will be lame. This condition tends to affect draught horses and is relatively un-common nowadays.

Causes
Injury or infection of the lateral cartilages.

Treatment
Call the vet to draw out the infection and give an antibiotic injection. As with a puncture wound, it is important that this wound heals from the inside out. Check that tetanus vaccinations are up to date.

Navicular syndrome

This condition is progressively degenerative in nature and

usually affects the navicular bones of both front feet. The exact causes are not definitely known — the condition rarely appears suddenly but tends to be insidious in onset. Often, because the condition and therefore the lameness is bilateral (occurs in both front feet), it may be well established before the owner is aware that there is a problem.

The condition occurs typically in horses between the ages of seven and twelve years and is most common in Thoroughbred crosses. It is very rare in pure bred Arabs or native ponies. Horses who have been subjected to high levels of work tend to be affected more frequently. It is thought that some cases of navicular are inherited, probably as a result of conformational defects.

The exact cause and mechanism of the condition is unknown. One theory is that it starts with a passive venous congestion which leads to thrombosis (clotting) of the arteries. This obstructs the flow of blood through the navicular bone, depriving the bone of essential nutrients and oxygen. This is known as ischaemia and results in the death of small areas of the bone. The deep digital flexor tendon passes over the back of the navicular bone, gliding on a pad of cartilage, before attaching to the lower aspect of the pedal bone. It applies pressure to the flexor surface of the navicular bone where the most significant lesions occur. Because of the impaired nutrition, the navicular bone remodels more quickly than normal and cartilage becomes ulcerated, pitted and roughened.

Signs

Characteristically, the lameness first shows periodically and lasts for a short time only. Sometimes the lameness wears off with exercise. Lameness may show up more clearly after approximately thirty minutes rest following strenuous exercise.

The stride gradually shortens — because this happens bilaterally it may not be noticed immediately.

The horse will tend to put the toe to the ground first before rapidly transferring his weight to the heel, resulting in a jarring appearance to the stride. The toe of the shoe will usually show signs of excessive wear. The shuffling gait often leads the owner to believe that the lameness is in the shoulder.

As the condition progresses, the periods of lameness increase in duration and become more frequent. The horse may be prone to stumbling—although stumbling in isolation is not considered a sign of navicular syndrome.

When observed in the stable, the horse may be seen trying to alleviate any pressure on the heels by standing with one toe pointing forwards. There may or may not be heat in the foot. He may shift his weight alternately from one foot to the other and dig up the bedding in order to stand with his heels raised on the mounds of bedding.

The digital blood vessels may be enlarged as they pass over the sesamoids but usually no increased pulsation is evident. By placing one's thumbs into the hollow of the heels and applying firm pressure, pain in the navicular area may be noted.

Occasionally, the condition may affect one forefoot only— possibly as the result of bearing extra strain at a time when the other foreleg was suffering some form of injury, such as tendon strain. A severely affected foot may appear smaller than the other healthy forefoot, because of contraction of the heels.

Diagnosis

Navicular syndrome is diagnosed on the clinical signs and confirmed by selective nerve blocking and x-ray. X-rays must be taken with the shoes off and the clefts of the frogs picked out to prevent 'shadows'. As changes on the flexor cortex are now thought to be the most significant, a new tangential view taken through the heel region should be included.

When tested for lameness, the horse suffering from navicular will normally demonstrate great discomfort upon continuous flexion of the fetlock and pastern joints. If trotted on immediately, he usually shows exaggerated lameness which gradually wears off.

Palmar digital nerve blocking will permit the horse to appear sound in the case of unilateral navicular syndrome. When both forefeet are affected, nerve blocking of one foot will accentuate the lameness of the other.

X-rays taken at approximately four-monthly intervals will show pathological changes in the navicular bone and confirm the presence of the condition. The changes observed include the formation of extra nutrient foramina. (The various tissues of the body, including bone, contain many openings known as foramen, through which pass other structures such as blood vessels and nerves.) In a normal working horse approximately five nutrient foramina, which should appear slightly conical in shape, may be seen along the flat lower edge of the navicular bone. In the diseased bone, new blood vessels try to break through and supply the deprived area, causing the existing foramen to become branch-shaped or rounded and also increasing the overall number of openings. On x-ray, changes in the shape of the foramina may be seen and any more than seven, or the appearance of foramina along the top or side edges, should be regarded as abnormal.

Causes

As opposed to there being one set cause, there are several factors which may predispose towards the onset of navicular syndrome. These factors include:

1) Enforced rest resulting in reduced movement, which may cause venous congestion within the foot.

2) Constant pressure on the navicular bone exerted by the deep digital flexor tendon which, in turn, compromises blood flow through the bone. This pressure may be increased when shoeing is neglected and the pastern/foot axis becomes too sloping.

3) Repeated compression and concussion from the frog below.

4) Hereditary defects such as conformation faults of the limbs, for example boxy feet or poor pastern/foot axis and, especially, excessively sloping pasterns, which put extra strain on the deep flexor tendons.

5) The formation of sidebones results in a loss of elasticity in the foot and impaired circulation.

Treatment

The pathological condition cannot be treated — any damage to the bone and cartilage is usually irreparable. Treatment is aimed at relieving the pain and trying to extend the horse's useful life. Treatments include:

Therapeutic shoeing. When shoeing a horse suffering from navicular the aims are to relieve the pressure on the deep digital flexor tendon by encouraging a straighter hoof/pastern axis, to promote improved circulation by increasing frog pressure and to ensure that the foot is properly balanced.

The farrier may place the shoe well back under the toe, with the heels extending round to the back of the frog. Some may advocate the use of bar shoes, in particular the oval-shaped egg-bar shoe which is currently being used with some success. Pads or wedges may be used to raise the heels, thus easing pressure on the tendons and helping to reduce concussion. The heels are generally encouraged to grow downwards which helps to straighten the hoof/pastern axis. It will be necessary to use rolled toes on the shoes to aid break-over.

Vasodilator therapy. Isoxsuprine hydrochloride is most effective in the very early stages of the disease, if the therapy begins immediately. Its main function is to widen blood vessels, thus allowing a free passage of blood. It is also thought to affect the viscosity of blood, acting as a thinning agent.

Anticoagulant therapy. One of the greatest breakthroughs in the treatment of navicular syndrome was the use of the anticoagulant drug, Warfarin. Warfarin reduces the viscosity of the blood, enabling it to flow through the affected vessels more easily, thus easing the state of thrombosis within the arteries. Because the treatment dose is close to the fatal dose, the dose rate has to be carefully calculated for each individual horse. The vet will take blood samples to ascertain the rate of the blood-clotting.

Once dosing has commenced, blood samples are taken regularly in order to monitor the effect and to ensure that the safe level is not exceeded — an overdose could lead to haemorrhaging. The treatment often lasts for nine to twelve months, in combination with corrective farriery and the introduction of regular exercise. Following this course of treatment, approximately 50 per cent of horses will stay sound. If lameness recurs, the treatment may start again.

Anti-inflammatory drugs and analgesics. Phenylbutazone (bute) has anti-inflammatory properties and is also analgesic (relieves pain). Of course, pain relief only masks the condition; it has no effect upon the degenerative process.

Another treatment is cortisone which, injected directly into the navicular bursa, may bring relief for between approximately three and six months.

More information about anti-inflammatory drugs and corticosteroids is given further on (Therapy to Reduce Inflammation).

Neurectomy. Generally considered to be a last resort, neurectomy or de-nerving involves surgically removing part of the nerves supplying the heel region of the foot. This allows the horse to work for a few more months but eventually nerves either regenerate or form painful nerve ending masses. Because of the way in which they grow back (in threadlike branches) the operation cannot normally be repeated.

A horse who has been 'de-nerved' must receive meticulous foot care as injuries such as puncture wounds may not be felt, and this can lead to infection and destruction of the foot structures without signs. FEI rules prohibit the use of neurectomized horses in competition.

A new treatment being researched involves cutting the suspensory ligaments of the navicular bone.

Pedal ostitis

This is demineralization of the pedal bone resulting from chronic inflammation.

The commonest form of pedal ostitis is caused by concussion, which leads to chronic bruising and inflammation of the pedal bone and sole. The symptoms include slight lameness and possibly a shortening of the forelimb stride on hard going — the horse will prefer working on soft ground rather than hard. X-rays will generally show changes in the appearance — the outline of the bone becoming more irregular.

Treatment involves shoeing to ensure a straight pastern/hoof axis. The farrier may recommend the use of a wide, flat shoe, the bearing surface of which is seated out to offer greater protection to the sole.

The other form of pedal ostitis is sometimes present in conjunction with navicular syndrome, small areas of porosis being present in the wings of the pedal bone.

Laminitis

Laminitis occurs as a result of several physiological changes which take place throughout the body, all culminating in a reduced blood flow through the sensitive laminae of the hoof wall.

Laminitis can affect both horses and ponies, but more commonly affects the latter. Research continues in an effort to determine why some animals are more susceptible to the condition than others and what exactly causes it.

Signs

The condition may affect any combination of fore or hind feet but, usually, both forefeet are involved. Often, but not always, the feet feel hot, particularly around the area of the coronet. The animal is normally reluctant to move, finding turning particularly difficult. He may shift his weight from foot to foot, and will resist attempts to have a foot lifted. The weight is borne on the heels with the hind feet well under the body and the forelegs extending forward. In severe cases the animal may sweat and his breathing quicken. He may lie down and be reluctant to stand.

There may be a rise in temperature, which could go as high as 106 °F (41 °C). The pulse rate may increase to between 80 and 120 per minute: the condition is extremely painful.

The blood pressure rises, causing changes in the blood flow to the feet. This is not yet fully understood as, although the increase in blood pressure causes increased blood flow to the feet, the blood flow through the sensitive laminae is decreased. It is thought that blood is 'shunted' from arterioles to venules without passing through the capillary bed of the laminae. There is a strong, bounding pulse in the digital arteries, level with the fetlock, partially the result of pain and the effect of the arterial blood reaching the obstructed vessels within the foot.

The capillary network within the sensitive laminae becomes congested with blood, the pooling of which results in the inefficient exchange of gases, leading to oxygen starvation in the tissue cells of the sensitive laminae. This deprivation causes damage to the tissue, the severity of which is dependent upon the duration of the disrupted blood flow. The damaged tissue swells, forcing the laminae away from the pedal bone. The weight of the horse bearing down on the pedal bone causes further separation. In severe cases, the pedal bone may rotate downward and press on the toe area of the sole. This pressure may eventually lead to the death of the tissue in the area (necrosis) which, if not corrected, may lead to the pedal bone penetrating the sole. If this occurs, the prognosis is extremely poor and euthanasia should be considered. Any damage to the tissue of the sole may then lead to secondary infection of the sensitive laminae ('seedy toe'). The rotation of the pedal bone may lead to a convex appearance of the sole and will cause severe lameness.

Causes

Although the exact causes are not fully known, laminitis may be divided into two categories:

Traumatic laminitis, in which the physiological changes are not the primary cause. For example, concussion may cause bruising and damage to the tissue of the sensitive laminae.

Systemic laminitis, which is caused through a culmination of physiological changes in the body.

There are many different factors which, in any combination, may cause a reduction in blood flow through the vessels of the sensitive laminae and trigger off systemic laminitis. Although horses can be sufferers, it has always been recognized that the 'fat pony on lush grass' is the most likely potential laminitis victim; physiological changes occur as a result of an imbalance in the metabolism. The factors which may bring about these physiological changes include:

1) The production of endotoxins. This may occur in several ways:

   (i) These toxins may be produced within the body as a result of a bacterial infection, for example after foaling there may be retention of the afterbirth leading to infection of the womb (endometritis).

   (ii) As a result of colic — endotoxins released from compromised gut in a strangulating lesion.

   (iii) Carbohydrate overload (from corn or spring grass). This alters the balance of bacteria within the caecum resulting in production of lactic acid. The change in pH kills some of the Gram-negative bacteria with the resultant release of endotoxins. These alter the gut wall and are absorbed into the bloodstream, resulting in laminitis.

   (iv) In liver disease. If, for some reason, the liver is damaged and not functioning properly, endotoxins may build up in the circulation, causing laminitis. A blood test would show raised liver enzymes.

2) Imbalances of calcium to phosphorous and of sodium to potassium. These imbalances are thought to affect the passage of electrochemical nerve impulses and could cause paralysis of the muscle of the arterial walls—this would exacerbate the problem of increased blood pressure. Moreover, the balance of minerals in the body affects the metabolism, therefore a general mineral deficiency may predispose to laminitis.

3) High doses of steroids (cortisone) increase the response of the digital blood vessels to circulating levels of adrenalin. This may result in 'shunting' and reduced blood flow to the foot.

The condition may be further complicated by secondary factors which include:

4) Sporadic intravascular coagulation — the pooling blood may clot in places, which further impedes the blood flow.

5) Changes in the levels of hormones produced by the endocrine glands. Marked changes in the levels of hormones including cortisol, testosterone, aldosterone, oestrogen, progesterone, renin and thyroxine could render the horse more susceptible to laminitis.

Treatment

Because of the serious nature of this ailment, the vet must be called for all but the mildest cases of laminitis. Mild may be interpreted as the signs being spotted and treated very quickly (same day) followed by rapid improvement (next day) and no reccurrence.

Treatment may be divided into three categories:

1) Removal of the primary cause
   (i)   In the case of the grass-kept horse, he must be stabled on-deep, non-edible bedding and fed only low feed-value hay and water. Obese animals should have their food intake reduced gradually to avoid liver damage. A mineral supplement may be given. The vet may provide a specially formulated supplement or advise as to the type of supplement one should purchase. Alternatively a mineral lick should be available at all times.
   (The school of thought at one time was to feed bran mashes. This is now known to interfere further with the calcium: phosphorous ratio. Bran contains a high level of phosphorous and bran fibre inhibits the horse's ability to utilize calcium. Whenever bran (or, indeed, any grain) is

fed limestone flour should be added to boost calcium levels).

(ii) In the event of any infection, the vet will prescribe and administer the necessary antibiotics. If an infection is suspected, particularly in connection with a broodmare, the vet must be called immediately. (If the afterbirth has not come away within six hours, the vet will administer oxytocin.)

(iii) If the horse has eaten a large quantity of feed, perhaps as result of escaping and gorging in the feed room, the vet may administer a solution of liquid paraffin and electrolytes via a stomach tube as a bulk laxative, in order to clear out the system.

(iv) A supplement high in methionine should be given to re-establish the depleted keratin sulphate of the laminae.

2) Correction of circulation

(i)   The high blood pressure is partially a result of the great pain so, for the comfort of the horse, relief from pain must be a priority. The vet will prescribe an analgesic. Although research has shown that bute can affect the metabolism of sodium and potassium, it is still the number one choice. Bute must only be administered to ponies under veterinary prescription. It is known to cause liver damage and other side-effects in certain breeds of pony. In endotoxaemic cases, a non-steroid anti-inflammatory drug such as flunixin may be given intravenously, followed by oral administration. Corticosteroid anti-inflammatories are contra-indicated as, for reasons unknown, they can actually *cause* laminitis and may make the situation worse. However, a single dose of cortisone may be administered intravenously on one day only. It is obviously important to be guided by the vet on current treatments for laminitis.

Another form of treatment which may be used is a drug to reduce blood pressure, thus easing the congestion within the foot. Such a drug will need regular administration. Vasodilators (drugs which widen the blood vessels) are now being used and in some cases proving beneficial. Anticoagulant therapy has also been used. Careful monitoring of clotting ability is essential.

Hosing or tubbing with *warm* water will help to relax and dilate the capillaries within the foot, so easing congestion. However, another traditional treatment, now known to generally aggravate the condition, is cold hosing. The application of cold water causes further vasoconstriction, impeding circulation. Nonetheless, in the very acute stage, cold hosing may assist insofar as it reduces the metabolic rate of the cells, and thus the demand for oxygen.

(ii)   If there are no signs of pedal bone rotation that is, if the laminits is of the mildest form, gentle walking in hand can be practiced. The walking will improve circulation, but must be carried out on a soft surface. Exercise in the acute stage is recommended by most vets if there are no signs of pedal bone rotation, and if it does not exacerbate the pain. However, if there are any indications that the pedal bone has started to rotate (the horse shows signs of pain upon pressure on the sole or the laminitis is beyond the very mild stage), the walking exercise would cause further tearing of the laminae, and pain. This pain would aggravate the high blood pressure, and the further damage to the laminae would cause greater rotation of the pedal bone. Therefore, in more severe cases, box rest will encourage the damaged laminitic tissue to repair, so preventing further rotation.

3) Prevention of pedal bone rotation

If the laminitis is at all prolonged (signs persist for longer than a few days), it will be essential to have the feet x-rayed to determine whether the pedal bone has rotated and, if so, by how much. The degree of pedal bone rotation can only be diagnosed through x-ray and only then can the vet and farrier plan a suitable programme of foot care. The most important factor to be considered when trying to prevent further rotation is that of resuming normal circulation. Having taken all of the

necessary steps, the vet will advise as to the shoeing require-
ments of the laminitic horse.

Once the stage of acute laminitis has passed, farriery can be
carried out. The wall of the hoof will have to be cut back and
the heel rasped down so as to realign the contours of the hoof
to the new position of the pedal bone (see Figure 29). Heart-
bar shoes offer support to the pedal bone and take the pressure
away from the toe, thus enabling the reattachment process to
proceed unhindered. The heart-bar shoe must be fitted accurately. There must be a small gap between the ground surface
of the frog and the 'V' section of the shoe to allow frog
movement.

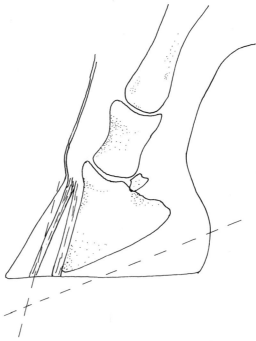

The broken lines show the desired contours of the wall — realigned with the
new position of the pedal bone.

Figure 29 Corrective farriery to reduce rotation of the pedal bone

Ringbone and sidebones

These ailments of the internal structures of the foot have been
discussed under the heading Bony Enlargements.

AILMENTS OF THE LOWER LEG

Sesamoiditis

Inflammation of the sesamoid bones.

Signs

Inflammation of the fetlock joint and lameness. If the fetlock joint is flexed for one or two minutes the horse will react, showing pain, and will trot up very lame.

Causes

Concussion and/or strain.

Treatment

Cold hosing and support bandaging may reduce swelling. Raised heels on shoes will reduce pressure on the fetlock joint. The vet may prescribe anti-inflammatory drugs and painkillers.

Sore (bucked) shins

Inflammation of the periosteum (bone membrane) at the front of the cannon bones of the foreleg.

Signs

Warm, painful swelling usually on the front of both cannon bones of the forelegs. Severe cases with excessive swelling are known as 'bucked shins'.

Causes

The condition is typically caused by concussion and is most usually observed in young Thoroughbreds in the early stages of training (two or three years) — it is not common in adult horses. As the horse works, pressure and concussive forces are exerted on the dorsomedial cannon bone, and remodelling takes place. If the remodelling cannot keep pace with the repeated compression stresses, bone failure occurs. Microfracture and subperiosteal haemorrhage result. Direct trauma, perhaps from a kick, can also cause sore shins.

Treatment

A minimum of one month's rest is essential, with cold treatments to reduce inflammation. Specialist treatments such as laser or magnetic field therapy may be recommended by vet/physiotherapist. The horse must be brought back into work in a controlled exercise programme to allow bone remodelling to keep up with the physical demands placed on the bone.

Osselet

Inflammation and exostosis on and around the fetlock joint.

Signs
Inflamed joint, distended appearance to the front of the fetlock caused by exostosis and excessive production of synovial fluid within the joint capsule. Pressure on the joint or flexion will cause pain. Lameness will be evident.

Causes
It is most commonly seen in young horse (two- and three-year-olds) and is caused by the effects of concussion on poor conformation and/or strained fetlock.

Treatment
X-ray to confirm diagnosis and determine severity, followed by rest and cold treatments.

Specialist treatments such as ultrasound and magnetic field therapy may assist—consult a specialist.

The appropriate treatment and *rest* are essential to prevent a vicious cycle of trauma and cartilage degeneration.

Tendon injury

The tendons of the lower limb are under varying degrees of pressure depending upon whether the horse is simply walking around a field or competing. Whatever work the horse is doing, the tendons are constantly changing—the old, worn fibres being replaced by new, young ones. Tendons are made up of bundles of collagen fibres which are arranged longitudinally and interspersed with collagen-producing cells known as fibroblasts.

Collagen is an inelastic fibrous protein which makes up the bulk of all skin, connective tissue, bone, cartilage and tendons. The type of collagen of which tendons are formed has a crimped structure which, if stretched, pulls straight, so helping to absorb and reduce stress and strain. As the collagen fibres become older and worn they lose their crimped effect, which results in a loss of elasticity.

The rate at which new collagen fibres replace old is dependent upon the adequate flow of blood bringing nutrients and oxygen to the area, and also correct pH levels. Blood circulation is increased and improved by regular exercise, therefore the collagen fibres are replaced more quickly, resulting in stronger tendons. The horse in less demanding work will not have such strong tendons, and should never be overexerted suddenly. Repeated loading of a tendon tends to stabilize its mechanical response, making it both more elastic and stiffer. In this state it is less susceptible to damage. This is why it is so important to warm up the horse gradually at the beginning of exercise.

Under normal healthy conditions the collagen in tendons should be renewed approximately every six months. However, interference with the oxygen supply, perhaps as a result of injury which impairs circulation, may lead to degenerative changes within the tendon, which will further complicate the healing process.

Signs of tendon injury

Early signs include localized heat and swelling — although the horse may not be lame initially. With more serious tendon strain there will be a greater degree of inflammation accompanied by severe lameness.

Causes of tendon injury

1) Muscle fatigue. Fatigue may result from bad going or the overexertion of an unfit horse. Once the parent muscle becomes fatigued it becomes less co-ordinated, placing extra strain on the tendon which may then be overstretched.

2) Conformation faults. Various conformation faults may cause or contribute to tendon injury:

(i) Long cannon bones will have long tendons, which are more susceptible to strain than shorter tendons.

(ii) Limbs which are too small in relation to the size of the body may not be strong enough to support it properly.

(iii) An excessively sloping pastern/foot axis exerts too much pressure on the tendons.

(iv) Mechanical injury may result from the horse striking into himself whilst jumping or galloping. (Such injury may also be the result of misfortune, for example, putting a foot down a rabbit hole).

(v) Degenerative injury. Poor circulation, and therefore poor oxygen supply, may be a result of faulty foot conformation. In such cases the collagen fibres are not replaced regularly. As previously described, the existing collagen loses its elasticity and is unable to withstand any level of stress. If subjected to regular stress, the warning signs of heat and swelling may appear.

(vi) Contracted tendons. As a result of contraction of the digital flexor tendons the heel may be raised and the fetlock joint straightened. In severe cases the front of the fetlock joint may even touch the ground. This condition, sometimes referred to as 'knocking over,' may be present at birth, in which case it may cause problems with foaling. Alternatively, it may develop suddenly in youngsters as a result of tendon injury, infection or dietary deficiency.

The effects of tendon injury

Depending upon the nature and extent of the injury, the tendon fibres are torn or stretched. This may lead to haemorrhaging within the tendon, which stimulates other cell-bearing fluids to enter the injured site. These fluids seep through from adjacent tissues in order to clear away debris such as dead tissue and to fight against infection of the damaged area.

As a result of cells dying, toxic substances are formed. These irritate the surrounding tissue and this further stimulates the flow of blood to the area, leading to inflammation (tendonitis). Where inflammation occurs beneath an annular ligament, extreme pressure is exerted on the inflamed area. This usually reduces circulatory flow, which can then lead to tissue death and bowed tendons ('low bow').

After an injury, the limb is usually naturally immobilized (the horse is reluctant to move) — this is a result of the pain and swelling. Further immobilization is enforced as the horse has to rest. This lack of movement leads to impaired circulation, as venous return is dependent upon muscle contraction. As a result of this the area becomes engorged with blood, fluids and cells, which solidify to form a haematoma.

In areas of intense inflammation, especially where a haematoma has formed, there is a danger of adhesions forming as a result of the loss of movement. Adhesions are areas where the healing tissues become stuck to over- and underlying tissues, which further limits movement. If adhesions are stretched, they break down and cause damage to adjacent areas.

In association with tendon fibre damage or as a reaction to an injury or blow, the tendon sheath may become inflamed. This is known as tenosynovitis.

The healing process

A few days after injury, new blood vessels begin to permeate the injured area, pushing their way through the engorged and swollen tissues. These blood vessels carry building cells for repair to the site, and also remove damaged tissue. The repair cells lay down collagen fibres to form a scar — sometimes referred to as granulation tissue. The repair collagen is not arranged longitudinally, but is placed in random fashion, which reduces the strength of the tendon. Eventually the fibres realign and are replaced, although the collagen with which they are replaced is of a weaker type. After a year or so this may again be replaced, this time with a stronger type of collagen.

Whenever dealing with tendon injuries it is necessary to bear in mind the time taken before the tendons are remodelled — in the year following injury the tendons will not be at full strength.

Treating tendon injuries

Although inflammation heralds the healing process the priority, for the reasons described above, is to immediately control and reduce it. Box rest will be essential in severe cases, to prevent the horse from using the limb and causing further damage. The vet may recommend that an accurate diagnosis to determine the severity of the injury be obtained through the use of ultrasound scanning equipment.

It is thought that controlled passive motion with slight tension on the injured tendon in the acute repair stage (granulation tissue deposition) helps with orientation of the fibrils and reduces adhesion formation. However, finding a balance between mild tension to promote repair and more severe tension which compromises healing, remains a problem.

Windgalls and Splints

These ailments of the lower leg have been discussed under the headings Bursal Enlargements and Bony Enlargements respectively.

AILMENTS OF THE UPPER FORELEG

'Broken knees'

Signs
The skin on the knees is damaged, varying from a mild graze to a deep puncture wound. If the tendon sheath or joint capsule is damaged, synovial fluid may escape and infection may enter the synovial structure, possibly leading to permanent incapacity.

Causes
The horse stumbling on a hard surface or falling onto his knees.

Treatment
Check the severity of the wound. Make sure you know how to recognize synovial fluid, if you should see it. Synovial fluid looks like thin honey — it is a clear, straw-coloured fluid which will form a mucin strand between separated fingers. If you see it, call the vet. If the wound is less severe, cleanse with cold running water and apply wound powder or cream.
Do not work the horse until the wound has healed properly; adjust diet and check on tetanus vaccinations.

Prevention

Keep feet regularly trimmed to prevent the toes from becoming overlong, since this can lead to stumbling. (Stumbling occurs more often in tired or unfit horses, so be particularly careful in these circumstances.)

Never ride on a long rein whilst out hacking and always fit knee boots when hacking on the road. Always travel the horse in knee boots.

Radial paralysis (dropped elbow)

Causes

Pressure on the musculo-spiral (radial) nerve, usually as it passes over the musculo-spiral groove (at lower front aspect) of the humerus. May be as a result of a kick, fall, fracture of the humerus or prolonged lying on one side.

Myositis (muscular inflammation) of the triceps will show a similar motornerve deficit.

Signs

The knee and fetlock on the affected limb are bent, with the elbow dropped and extended. The horse is unable to bear weight or advance the limb.

Skin sensation to the front outside portion of the forearm is lost.

These signs occur because the radial nerve carries the motor supply to the extensors of the forelimb, the lateral flexor of the knee and the sensory supply to the front outer aspect of the forearm — functions which are lost when the nerve becomes paralysed.

Treatment

Consult the vet. Electrical stimulation of the nerve tissue will help prevent atrophy and massage will help improve circulation. It is important to prevent contraction of the flexors of the lower limb.

Capped knees and elbows

These injuries have been discussed under the heading Bursal Enlargements.

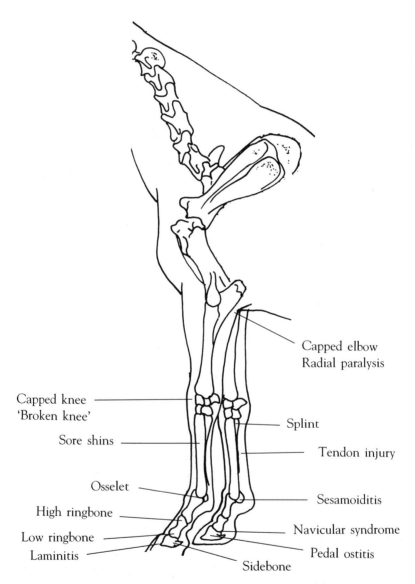

Figure 30 Locations of the various causes of lameness

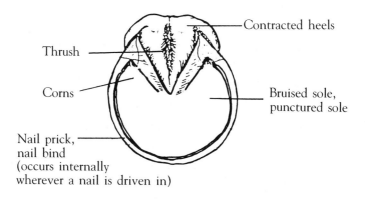

Contracted heels

Thrush

Corns

Bruised sole, punctured sole

Nail prick, nail bind (occurs internally wherever a nail is driven in)

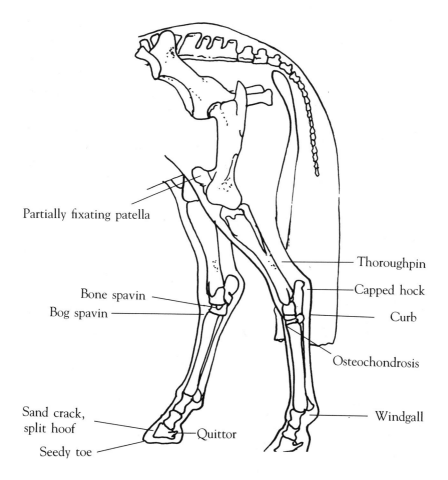

Partially fixating patella

Bone spavin

Bog spavin

Thoroughpin

Capped hock

Curb

Osteochondrosis

Sand crack, split hoof

Seedy toe

Quittor

Windgall

AILMENTS OF THE UPPER HIND LEG

Partially fixating patella

The stifle joint corresponds to the human knee joint, and the patella corresponds to the human kneecap. Should the patella deviate from its normal position the joint may lock, forcing the limb to be held up in an abnormal way.

The normal locking mechanism, which the horse uses to rest standing up, involves locking the middle patellar ligament over the medial trochlear ridge of the femur. In upwards fixation, the patella becomes locked upwards and the releasing mechanism does not function properly. There is thought to be an hereditary basis for this, with conformation playing a significant role. Trauma and poor muscling (unfitness) may also contribute.

If increasing the horse's fitness does not relieve the condition, the vet may need to operate on the tendons and ligaments of the joint.

It is also possible, though rare, for the patella to become dislocated — this is sometimes referred to as a slipped stifle. The dislocation may be caused by leading a horse carelessly through a partially opened stable door or gateway.

The vet will be needed to correct the dislocation, reduce inflammation and promote muscle stimulation.

Curb, thoroughpin, bog spavin and capped hock

These injuries have been discussed under Bursal Enlargements.

Bone spavin

This has been discussed under Bony Enlargements.

AILMENTS OF THE JOINTS

Synovitis

Inflammation of the synovial membrane lining a joint cavity. The membrane becomes thickened and secretes an excessive amount of synovial fluid into the joint. The condition may be referred to as capsulitis.

Signs
The joint is hot, painful and swollen, and may be kept flexed with the toe resting on the ground. The degree of lameness will be determined by the extent of the inflammation. In chronic cases the symptoms persist. Synovitis may be closely associated to bursitis (see below).

Causes
Injury, infection. Bursal enlargements tend to be a result of chronic synovitis.

Treatment
Cold treatments may help alleviate the condition.
Consult a specialist regarding ultrasound, magnetic field or similar therapies.
If synovitis results from infection, the vet may flush the joint and will administer antibiotics. It is important to reduce inflammation and flush out the infected joint because by-products of the inflammatory response and bacterial toxins are destructive to the articular cartilage. If untreated, degenerative joint disease (DJD) will ensue. (This condition is dealt with further on.)

Bursitis

Inflammation of a bursa.

Signs
Thickening of a bursa, for example around the elbow, knee and

hock joints (see Bursal Enlargements).
May initially cause lameness, but often does not. As with synovitis, degree of lameness depends upon the extent of inflammation.

Causes
Strain, injury, infection.

Treatment
As for synovitis.

Arthritis and degenerative joint disease

Arthritis is defined simply as inflammation of the joint. It is a non-specific term which may involve synovitis and/or be degenerative in nature. This latter term is often used synonymously with degenerative joint disease.

Signs
Inflamed joint; difficulty in flexing the affected joint, giving a stiff appearance. If prolonged, may become osteoarthritis (see below).

Causes
Infection, injury, nutritional imbalance (mineral deficiency), old age. It may also be secondary to other disorders, as is the case with degenerative joint disease (DJD). This, sometimes referred to as osteoarthritis or arthrosis, is a degenerative condition resulting in the destruction of cartilage. This ultimately affects all the tissues of the joint.

DJD is the most common joint disease encountered. It may occur as a result of synovitis, ringbone, insidious 'wear and tear', cartilage damage, or be secondary to bone fracture within joints, dislocations, wounds, infective arthritis, osteochondrosis (see later) etc.

Adult cartilage is composed of an organic matrix of collagen and glycoproteins. Collagen provides tensile strength; glyco-proteins provide compressive stiffness. The main lubricant contained in both cartilage and synovial fluid is hyaluronic acid. DJD causes chemicals to be released into the joint which cause the production of more synovial fluid and reduce the levels of hyaluronic acid. The joint surface becomes ulcerated and the underlying bone becomes reactive and more dense (sclerotic). In highly mobile joints (such as fetlock, hock and knee) changes are first seen near the joint margins and small bony projections (osteophytes) develop.

Treatment

The severity of the condition can be determined by x-ray. The vet will treat the cause of the arthritis, for example, if it is a result of infection, he will administer suitable antibiotics.

Phenylbutazone (bute) may be prescribed to reduce inflammation and ease pain, or cortisone may be injected directly into the affected joint.

Two drugs used effectively to treat DJD are Hylartil and Adequan.

Hylartil (hyaluronic acid), injected into the joint suppresses inflammation, improves synovial membrane function and replaces hyaluronic acid which has been broken down by the inflammatory response. It may prevent further cartilage damage but will not help repair existing damage.

Adequan (polysulphated glycosaminoglycan), injected either intramuscularly or into the joint, inhibits destructive enzymes within the joint and promotes synthesis of hyaluronic acid. It is used in active synovitis and prevents cartilage degeneration.

Other factors to be considered in the treatment of arthritis and DJD are:

Cease all hard work to allow the soft tissue inflammation to subside. (Although gentle walking in hand and passive joint manipulation may be beneficial.)

Consult a specialist on the use of ultrasound, magnetic field therapy or similar.

Cider vinegar mixed with cod liver oil may be added to the diet and does, in some cases, bring about improvement.

Corrective shoeing (raised heels and rolled toes) can ease strain on joints and improve break-over.

Other specific forms of arthritis are:

Ankylosing arthritis. In this form, destruction of the joint surfaces causes the underlying bones to become fused, thus preventing movement (ankylosis). If this involves a low-motion joint (for example, bone spavin at a distal intertarsal joint), the lameness disappears once the ankylosis is complete. In a high-motion joint, however, crippling lameness may result, requiring veterinary opinion as to the benefits of carrying out treatment.

Infective arthritis is sometimes referred to as joint-ill or, if more than one joint is involved, polyarthritis. It is caused by bacteria gaining entry to the joints. In foals, the bacteria mainly enter via the navel and travel in the blood to the joint; in adult horses entry may be via a puncture wound. Treatment involves flushing the joint with saline solution and extensive use of antibiotics to fight the infection, as the bacteria cause the joint surfaces to erode.

Osteochondrosis

Osteochondrosis is a disturbance of conversion of cartilage to bone during bone formation, resulting in persistence of cartilage in the area under the articular cartilage.

There may be separation of a fragment of articular cartilage and underlying bone. Such a fragment, referred to as a joint mouse, causes pain and varying degrees of lameness. Where such a fragment is present, the condition is referred to as osteochondrosis dissecans (OCD).

Signs
The condition is most commonly seen in one or both stifle or hock joints of young horses.

Osteochondrosis may show inflammation, stiffness and/or lameness.

Diagnosis will be confirmed by x-ray.

Treatment

If inflammation is present, anti-inflammatory therapy will be required. Because of the need for analgesia, phenylbutazone may be prescribed.

Where there is a fragment, surgery to remove it may be necessary to avoid development of DJD. In other cases, treatment is with rest and anti-inflammatories.

The long-term outcome depends upon whether or not DJD develops.

LIMB FRACTURE

A bone may fracture upon being subjected to a particular force or stress. In the horse, this may occur as a result of a kick, fall, blow, putting a foot down a hole whilst cantering or some similar accident. Although all bones are susceptible to fracture, those most commonly affected in the horse are the long pasterns, cannon bones, pedal bones, sesamoids and splint bones.

Developments in modern veterinary surgery including the use of rigid internal fixation, bone grafting techniques, improved anaesthetic procedures and better casting materials have generally improved the prognosis for a limb fracture. However, the outcome of any injury will depend upon the following factors:

Which bone is fractured.

The nature of the fracture.

The nature of other associated injuries.

The initial management of the fracture at the scene of the accident.

The age and temperament of the horse.

Finances, insurance cover and value of the horse.

The usefulness of the horse upon recovery.

Types of fracture

Fractures are classified according to the type of break — this range of classifications is very extensive. To the layman, the broad categories are more relevant, and it is these we shall discuss.

Simple fracture. This is the most common type. The bone is broken clean across, and the break is described as transverse, longitudinal or oblique, according to its direction. There may be damage to surrounding tissue.

Compound fracture. The skin is damaged and the break is exposed. This is a very serious injury, which may be prone to heavy bleeding and infection.

Comminuted fracture. There is a lot of splintering, involving a number of pieces of bone.

Incomplete fracture. The bone breaks partly across but the periosteum (bone membrane) generally does not break. This is also known as a 'greenstick' fracture and may occur in young foals whose bones are still immature.

Signs
Loss of use of limb.

No weight-bearing on limb.

Deformity of limb.

Unnatural mobility of limb.

Apparent shortening of length of limb.

Pain and swelling.

Crepitus — grating sound as bone endings move.

Initial management of a fracture

First aid measures must be taken at the scene of an accident to prevent further deterioration of the injury. The outcome of many fractures is determined by the success of this initial treatment. The limb must be very well padded and supported to help minimize the effects of the injury and to reduce subsequent damage. Unless stabilized, closed fractures may become open and damaged soft tissue will be susceptible to infection and a localized loss of blood supply (ischaemia). If the fracture is open, antibiotic therapy must start immediately, although the prognosis is not good, especially if there is little tissue covering the bone, or the wound has been contaminated.

To make up the heavily padded splints that are required, 5 kg of cotton wool or similar, five rolls of gauze bandages and ten elasticated bandages are needed. In an emergency, when no specialized splints are available, PVC guttering or wooden tool handles may be used to provide stability. The cotton wool is wrapped around the limb and compressed with tight gauze bandaging. The elastic bandages are then applied and the splints strapped tightly to the outside. The splints should not extend beyond the padding.

The joint above and below the break should be immobilized. This is difficult if the fracture is above the knee or hock, because it is impossible to bandage the stifle or elbow satisfactorily. It is not wise to attempt to splint these joints as that could cause displacement of the fracture.

The sound limb will require a support bandage because it will be bearing much extra weight. A lot of pain will occur as a result of the bone ends moving—immobilization will help to alleviate this. (In addition to keeping the bone ends still, immobilization is crucial in that the blood supply for the healing process comes from the soft tissue and endosteum and, if this is not preserved, repair is compromised.) The vet will administer painkillers, but will judge the level of analgesia carefully as the horse must not be encouraged to use the limb.

Generally, the use of sedatives is avoided because of their effect on the cardiovascular system. A horse suffering from shock and haemorrhage will react adversely to any lowering of arterial blood pressure. Also, sedatives may lead to incoordination which could result in further injury, especially during transit. However, in some circumstances a sedative *has* to be administered to prevent the horse from inflicting further damage, or to facilitate removal from the site of the accident. In such cases a short-acting agent such as xylazine may be administered intravenously by the vet.

Once the temporary stabilization of the limb is complete and all other first aid measures have been attended to, the horse can be moved to the veterinary clinic for a thorough examination. An ambulance trailer with a low, flat ramp will be required. The horse must be supported with a sling; if none is available, it may be necessary to improvise with straw bales.

The healing process

The healing of a fracture involves a complex sequence of changes; a number of different stages which overlap.

Haemorrhage. Bleeding occurs at the site of fracture as a result of the rupture of blood vessels in the periosteum, bone marrow and adjacent tissues. A large number of white blood cells will converge at the area.

Haematoma formation. The haemorrhage coagulates and envelopes the bone endings. The fragments of bone and connective tissue degenerate and are removed by phagocytes (white blood cells, which adhere to and destroy invading bacteria). The haematoma then undergoes organization and is replaced by granulation tissue, forming a fibrous callus with non-aligned collagen fibres.

Fibrous callus. Fibroblasts (collagen-forming cells) produce many collagen fibres, which mainly lie parallel to the long axis of the bone. The callus anchors and seals the break by surrounding it. Tissue between the bone endings unites the break and further callus encircles it — this is known as bridging.

Ossification. The fibrous tissue is transformed into 'woven' bone by osteoblasts (bone-forming cells) forming a thick ring of new bone referred to as hard callus. The bone first produced is immature (spongy) and is later replaced by adult (lamellar) bone. When union is complete the thick ring of bone is remodelled. If the break does not heal well the new ring of bone will remain to provide strength.

General considerations in fracture treatment

The main aim is to restore full use of the damaged limb as soon as possible. Prolonged immobilization will lead to various problems including joint stiffness, muscle atrophy, impaired circulation and soft tissue adhesions. There will also be a risk of poor bony adhesions resulting in a malunion of the broken limb and excessive callus formation.

Fractures in foals tend to repair more successfully than in the adult horse because they are smaller, therefore the bones bear less weight. Also the bone-producing cells are still very active, which promotes faster healing.

Fixation techniques

The aim is to provide a primary union rather than a large callus that has to be remodelled. The fractured limb needs to be rigidly immobilized in order to realign the bone ends properly. This may be achieved using either internal or external fixation techniques.

Internal fixation

Performed under general anaesthetic, the aim of internal fixation is to produce forces between bone endings/fragments in order to minimize any movement at the fracture line. This is achieved by using screws with or without plates, or, less commonly, by tension band wiring.

Lag screws and/or compression plates exert the pressure necessary to maintain compression of the bone fragments, so reducing movement. Tension band wiring is a technique whereby increased tension is exerted on the screws or plates.

External fixation

External fixation — the use of a rigid cast to immobilize the limb, may provide additional strength and reinforcement to internal implants, or may be the sole means of support. An example of the latter is that external fixation is often used for communited fractures that cannot be immobilized with internal fixation techniques.

The cast must immobilize the joint above and below the break. The cast should not finish mid-shaft of the radius or tibia, as pressure sores may result. When casting a lower limb injury, the foot should be included to prevent sores on the coronet.

Full limb casts are usually applied under general anaesthetic. All shoes are removed and the sole of the contralateral foot may be filled with acrylic to help prevent the possibility of pedal bone rotation, which may occur as a result of that limb bearing so much extra weight for such a great length of time.

The wound is covered in an antibiotic-impregnated sterile dressing before two layers of stockinette are applied. Special care is taken around potential pressure areas, for example the back of the knee. Excessive padding is avoided as it may compress, causing the cast to become loose. The limb is then bandaged with the casting material—new materials have generally replaced plaster of paris. Polyurethane resins impregnated on polyester or fibreglass bandages provide a strong and light cast. They are more durable, less susceptible to deterioration and can be x-rayed. A full cast applied to a forelimb is generally set in a natural weight-bearing position. In the hind limb, the fetlock and pastern may be slightly flexed. Further limb supports may be bandaged in.

Provided that there are no complications, the cast may remain unchanged for up to six weeks. It must, however, be checked daily for warm spots and cracking. If the initial cast is applied to a swollen limb it will require changing as soon as the swelling subsides. Later on, muscle atrophy and general weight loss may cause the cast to become loose, and it will need replacing.

The sound limbs must be bandaged for support. These

bandages must be removed at least twice daily and the limbs massaged before the bandages are re-applied.

Some pressure sores are inevitable and, if superficial, will heal once the cast is removed. If the cast is too tight it could interfere with circulation causing necrosis, (tissue death). This is a very serious condition and, if severe, would necessitate the destruction of the horse.

Great forces are applied to the limbs as a horse rises after lying down. Therefore, if temperament permits, a horse suffering from limb fracture may be tied up to prevent him from lying down.

With an injury as serious as a limb fracture, the owner must constantly be advised by the veterinary surgeon and his team as to the daily progress and care of the horse.

6

THERAPIES TO REDUCE INFLAMMATION

Methods of controlling inflammation include:

Cold therapy.

Hydrotherapy.

Heat therapy.

Therapy machines which facilitate treatments such as magnetic field therapy, ultrasound, laser, Electrovet, Ionicare and faradic therapy.

Massage.

Support.

Anti-inflammatory drugs.

The exact treatment given immediately will depend upon the nature of the injury. If a horse has struck into himself there will be an open wound to deal with. Any bleeding must be stopped and the wound thoroughly cleaned.

COLD THERAPY/HYDROTHERAPY

Cold treatments can be used immediately after injury. The effects on the injured tissues include:

Vasoconstriction. The blood vessels tighten and so blood flow is reduced. This helps to control the formation of haematomas (blood-filled swelling) and oedema (fluid accumulation in tissues) beneath the skin. Vasoconstriction also assists in stopping bleeding in an open wound.

Vasodilation. This has been found to occur in the deep tissues of the area in response to the intense cold when ice treatments are in place for ten minutes or more. Vasodilation follows vasoconstriction, which has the effect of increasing circulatory flow through the area.

Analgesia. As circulation is generally improved inflammation is reduced, so easing the pain.

Easing of muscle spasm. As pain is reduced so muscle spasm begins to ease. Muscles go into spasm in reaction to pain — the tightness of this spasm further heightens the pain and interferes with the circulatory flow which, in turn, reduces the oxygen supply to the area. Any interference with the supply of oxygen may lead to degenerative changes and tissue death.

Hosing

The most common practice, hosing, should be carried out for approximately twenty minutes at least three times daily. The heels must be plugged with Vaseline and carefully dried after hosing to prevent cracking. It is possible to buy specially designed 'hose boots' which enable the horse to be left standing and thus save time spent holding the hosepipe. Great care is needed as the sole and frog quickly become soaked and the horn softens excessively. Iodine-based medications help prevent this. Some of the aquaboots compress the water jets, giving a jacuzzi-type massage. This reduces oedema and improves circulation.

Cold tubbing

A sturdy container is filled with cold water and crushed ice. The horse then has to be encouraged to stand with the injured limb immersed for approximately fifteen minutes, two or three times a day. Precautions must again be taken to prevent cracked heels — pack heels with Vaseline and dry carefully afterwards.

Cold water bandages

In this traditional treatment, a bandage and gamgee are soaked in icy water and put into position. This dressing must be checked and replaced frequently, as the water soon warms up. Alternatively, pour ice water through the dressing regularly. Under no circumstances should the bandages be allowed to dry out on the limb, because of the risk of shrinkage.

Ice treatments

Because of the risk of ice burn, ice treatments must not be placed in direct contact with the skin. A layer of lint or similar material should be placed between the ice pack and the skin. Prolonged exposure to intense cold may lead to ischaemia (tissue death as a result of reduced blood flow). Also, because of the vasoconstriction of the superficial blood vessels, traditional ice treatments must not be in position for longer than thirty minutes on any one area. However, there are various types of specialist preparations available on the market. These include gel-filled sachets and bandages impregnated with gel which, once frozen, remain cold for up to three hours. These preparations are designed to reach a therapeutic temperature level, so may be used safely without the risk of tissue death.

More traditionally, gamgee may be soaked and frozen in the deep freeze. This can then be bandaged in position. The ice particles begin to melt once the dressing is in place. Another useful form of cold poultice is kaolin spread between two sheets of polythene and then frozen. This makes an economic, reusable cold dressing.

It is a good idea to keep one or two ice treatments ready-frozen.

HEAT THERAPY

Heat therapy should not be used if severe infection of the deeper tissues is suspected, since vasodilation can cause the spread of toxins. Nor should it be used in advance of other therapies (such as the administration of antibiotics) which may act to treat, and thus reduce, the infection. However, the *localized* application of heat (as in poulticing and hot tubbing) can be useful in drawing out pus resulting from local, relatively mild, infection.

Heat lamps

Back injury involving muscle spasm will respond favourably to the application of superficial heat. This is facilitated through the use of infra-red and/or ultra-violet lamps (solaria). These may be purchased as either mobile or static units. The manufacturers' instructions regarding usage and duration should be followed.

Heat lamps should be suspended at such a height that they are effective, yet cannot burn the horse. The horse should be tied up and unrugged beneath the lamps, and should not be able to touch either the lamps or the wires. The duration of treatment will depend upon the nature of the condition. Approximately thirty minutes, two or three times daily should greatly benefit the horse. After heat treatments such as these, the horse should remain rugged up in his box to rest.

Short-wave diathermy

The deep tissues of the body (including bone) can be warmed by means of a machine emitting a high-frequency alternating current. Because damage can easily occur through overheating of the deep tissues, this machine must only be used by a qualified person. It should never be carried out if bone screws or metalware are in place.

Poultices

Poultices help to relieve bruising, clean wounds, draw out infection and reduce inflammation.

To prevent burning, always ensure that poultices are not too hot when applied; test the temperature on the back of your hand. Common types of poultice are:

Animalintex, a ready prepared lint dressing which you simply cut to size and soak in very hot water. Wring out the excess water, apply to the injury and cover with polythene. Either bandage into position using gamgee as padding or, if using on an area where bandaging is impractical, hold in place with waterproof sticking plaster. Animalintex may also be used as a cold dressing. The method of applying a poultice to a wound in the foot has been described earlier (Punctured sole).

Kaolin, a paste which is heated up in its tin — prise the lid loose and stand in a saucepan of boiling water. The paste may be spread on unbroken skin to reduce swelling, for example after a kick. Always test the temperature of kaolin carefully — it can get very hot. When it is at the desired temperature, spread onto a piece of sterile cloth, such as lint and stick directly onto the swelling, covering with gamgee held in position with sticking plaster.

Bran. If Animalintex is not available, hot bran makes a useful substitute when dealing with a wound of the foot. Make up a small bran mash adding 50 g (2 oz) of Epsom salts. The Epsom salts add to the drawing properties of the poultice. Place the bran in a stout polythene bag and place over the foot so that the injured area is covered with the wet, hot bran. Pad over with gamgee and bandage as previously described, using either a poultice boot or hessian sacking for additional protection. There are several types of poultice or Equiboot available. The boot provides a stronger and more effective method of protecting the poultice than hessian sacking.

Hot tubbing

This is a form of treatment to ease bruising of the lower leg, to draw out infection and clean puncture wounds. You will need a strong rubber bucket full of hot (not *too* hot) water and Epsom salts. Place Vaseline in the heels, pick out and scrub the foot, then immerse the injured limb. The horse must be encouraged to stand still with his foot in the bucket. Add hot water regularly and keep the foot immersed for twenty minutes. Repeat at least twice daily.

Fomentation

Hot and cold fomentations can be used to help reduce swelling. To do this you need a bucket of very cold water, two small hand towels and a bucket of very hot water. Keep the kettle hot so that you can top up the hot water. Soak each towel and wring out the cold one. Hold this over the bruise for a minute or two, then wring out the very hot towel and hold that over the bruise. Repeating the alternate hot and cold applications will stimulate the circulation by causing the blood vessels to dilate then constrict. The blood and fluid which has gathered beneath the skin should start to disperse. You will need to do this for at least twenty minutes three times a day until the bruising has eased.

THERAPY MACHINES

A wide range of specialist therapies is now available for the treatment of lameness. These therapies are in use by physiotherapists and other expert personnel at clinics and rehabilitation centres. Many of the machines are available to purchase, but it must be stressed that they should be used *in accordance with the vet's or physiotherapist's advice and only by a trained person.* Furthermore, the information given below regarding the various machines and treatments should not be considered a substitute for the advice of an equine specialist. Advice must always be sought promptly for diagnostic and therapeutic purposes in the

case of injury and/or lameness. Delay may lead to irreparable damage and permanent unsoundness.

Magnetic field therapy

Much research has gone into the effects of pulsating and static magnetic field therapy in the treatment of both hard (bone) and soft (muscle and tendon) tissue damage. Certain pulses of magnetic field improve circulation, which increases cell activity, so promoting the healing process. Research suggests that different pulses affect different tissues.

Pulsating magnetic field therapy may be administered through a mains operated machine or, if treating a leg injury, through a battery operated boot. Static magnetic field therapy is administered through the use of magnetic foil which remains in place almost continually.

The manufacturers give full treatment instructions which, together with the advice of an expert, should be followed carefully.

Ultrasound

Sound may be defined as vibrating waves travelling through a medium such as air. The length, velocity and frequency of sound waves are measured in cycles per second, which are expressed as hertz. A kilohertz (KHz) is 1000 cycles per second; a megahertz (MHz) is 1 million cycles per second. The normal limit of human hearing is around 20 KHz. Ultrasound waves cannot be perceived by the human ear as they have a frequency well above this.

Ultrasonic waves are reflected by air; it causes them to bounce back upon themselves. However, when emitted from an ultrasound machine used by a trained person, ultrasonic waves may be used for scanning tissue for measurement, diagnosis and treatment.

When used as treatment, ultrasound waves are converted to heat in the tissues. The treatment is best used for deep heat penetration of muscles (to treat myositis) and for nerve damage, tendon injury, bursitis and scars. Blood flow is increased, helping to reduce inflammation and muscle spasm, and scar tissue may become more elastic after ultrasound treatment.

It is not of value in cases of bone damage, and can actually damage bone. For this reason, it should not be used over the spine. Furthermore, it should not be used in acute injuries (as it may cause haematoma formation) or over metal implants or recent surgical sites. Also, if ultrasound is used for too long, at too high a temperature, by an inexperienced person, damage may occur within the deep structures.

Ultrasound machines

These machines, originally designed for human usage, may have three frequency settings; 0.75 MHz, 1 MHz and 3 MHz. However, the most commonly used machines often have only the 1 MHz setting, which makes them less controllable when treating structures of differing depths.

The machines are mains operated, the generator being within an earthed metal box on which are the control dials. The dials control the setting of timing, intensity (ultrasonic waves are measured as watts/cm^2) and whether the waves are pulsed or continuous. Attached to the generator by a lead is the transducer, or treatment head. Attached to the metal plate of the transducer is a special type of crystal (usually quartz or barium titnate) which is capable of vibrating according to the setting of the machine (thus, at 1 MHz the crystal must vibrate at 1 million cycles per second). The high frequency current is transmitted from the crystal to the metal plate, which produces an ultrasonic wave. This wave has to pass through a medium other than air — a special coupling gel may be used or, in treating a limb, the affected area may be immersed in water.

When used for diagnostic purposes, the emitter and receiver are in a probe. Depending upon the depth of penetration needed, a setting of 3, 5 or 7.5 MHz is used.

Method of treatment

The area to be treated is clipped closely. If the immersion method is being used, the affected limb is submerged in a strong tub of water. All air bubbles must be rubbed out of the hair, so that the ultrasound waves are not reflected back. The treatment head is held parallel to the limb approximately

1−2 cm away and moved in a slow circular or parallel motion.

If the contact method is to be used, the treatment surface of the transducer and the area to be treated should be well covered in the coupling gel. The transducer is placed firmly onto the area to be treated and the machine timing and intensity set. As the beam travels through the coupling medium and the tissues of the body, its intensity is reduced. The effect of this is calculated and taken into account when treating the deeper structures. The lower the wattage per cm^2, the better. Damage may occur if the treatment sessions are continued over too long a period.

With the contact method of treatment, the transducer head is moved in the same way as with the immersion method. This head should always be kept in motion to avoid overheating the tissue.

Laser

The word laser is an acronym: Light Amplification by Stimulated Emission of Radiation. Laser apparatus emits a beam of intense light which may be used for surgical, healing and/or analgesic purposes dependent upon the type of laser used.

High power or hot lasers actually destroy tissue through intense heat and have been used in various forms of surgery with success.

Low power or cold lasers do not destroy tissue, but have great therapeutic values.

When treatment is being given with a low power laser, the laser beam may be emitted in a pulsed or continuous wave; a pulsed beam is effective for analgesic purposes, while a continuous beam is generally used for healing.

Laser has an analgesic effect when used correctly on the acupuncture points. This treatment must be carried out approximately once a week by a trained person familiar with the many acupunture points.

If a continuous beam is used on an open wound, it penetrates the tissues and is absorbed by the cells, where it acts as an extra energy source. This extra energy accelerates the healing process by helping collagen to be produced more rapidly.

Laser has been used to treat superficial joint and bone injuries, tendon and ligament conditions and old fibrous scar tissue. This treatment reduces the time taken to recover quite noticeably, even though there is no sensation felt by the horse while the beam is penetrating the damaged tissues.

Laser is generally effective to a depth of 10−15 mm, the depth of penetration and the effectiveness of the beam being dependent on the wavelength of the emitted beam frequency. The apparatus should only be used by a trained and skilled operator, as used wrongly laser may have adverse effects on the injured site. Also, because of the risk of eye damage, it is important not to look directly at the laser source. There is still much research being carried out in the field of laser therapy.

Electrovet and Ionicare units

All cell membranes consist of electrically charged particles known as ions. After injury to any specific area the ionic balance of the tissue is disturbed, resulting in impaired transmission of nervous impulses and varying degrees of loss of function. The functions can only be restored fully when any ionic imbalance has been rectified. Once the nervous impulses are travelling in the normal manner, the muscles will receive stimulation — without stimulation muscle deteriorates, becoming atrophied.

There are two main types of machine devised to restore the correct ionic balance within the cells. These are the Electrovet and Ionicare systems. Both units consist of a surcingle containing a negative electrode. A pack mounted on the surcingle holds a small electrical generator which is run by rechargeable batteries. To be effective, the generator must be fully charged before use. The surcingle is buckled firmly into position over a folded towel and the control dial adjusted to either the 'leg' or 'muscle' setting.

The electrodes used to stimulate the injured area are covered in a special coupling gel and the area soaked with water.

Electrodes on the leg may be held in position with bandages; those on the body may be hand-held. The leads from the machine to the electrodes are then connected, followed by the lead from the generator to the negative electrode on the surcingle. The machine operator will then slowly turn up the control dial until the horse indicates, by quivering or lifting the limb, that he can feel the current. The machine is then adjusted as appropriate and left on for approximately two hours. During this time the horse may stand tied up, with a haynet to keep him occupied. Once the equipment has been disconnected and removed, the treated area should be carefully washed and dried to avoid irritation of the skin.

Depending on which setting is chosen the machines are useful in the treatment of tendon and joint damage, bursal enlargements, muscle strain and atrophied muscle. According to the instructions of the vet or physiotherapist, the overall treatment usually lasts for about three weeks.

Faradism

Faradism is the term often used to describe the artificial stimulation of muscle tissue with an electric current. Specialist training is essential as a deep knowledge of the muscles, their functions and their motor points is essential if faradism is to be of true benefit to the horse.

By means of a faradic machine the muscles may be stimulated with an electric (faradic) current, which will cause the muscle fibres to contract. As they do so, their strength may be developed, thus preventing further atrophy. The movement of the muscle fibres also helps to keep the formation of scar tissue and adhesions to a minimum. Another benefit is that electrical stimulation improves venous and lymphatic flow, which results in improved circulation and reduced inflammation.

The easiest machine to use is the battery operated type which may be strapped around the operator's waist for ease of movement, with the active electrode being hand-held. A faradic machine has two leads which have electrodes at one end. One is the active electrode and the other is termed indifferent. The electrodes and the area to be treated are soaked with a saline solution which acts as a good conductor of the electrical current. The electrodes generally consist of thin metal plates which must not come into direct contact with the skin — a thin layer of padding helps prevent irritation. The area to be treated may be covered in coupling gel so that the active electrode can glide over the hair when moved from one motor point to another. A motor point is the place at which a motor nerve enters a muscle and branches off into a network of smaller nerves. It is at these points that stimulation should be directed to achieve maximum muscle contraction.

The indifferent electrode is strapped onto an area just behind the withers by means of a roller and pad. The most comfortable sensation is felt by the horse when the roller is firmly done up. The operator has the machine fastened around the waist with all controls switched off. The lead from the indifferent pad is attached to the machine. The lead from the hand-held active pad is then also attached to the machine and positioned on the relevant motor nerve. The trained operator will judge the necessary speed of the muscle contraction required (the surge) and the intensity of the electrical stimulus and adjust the dials accordingly. The muscle is then stimulated some twenty to thirty times before moving on to the next muscle. The muscle must not be overstimulated — fatigue may occur if it is not allowed to rest.

Electrical stimulation of muscle may also be used for diagnostic purposes. This is achieved by comparing the reactions of healthy and the corresponding unhealthy muscles. The horse may show signs of pain when a damaged muscle is stimulated. Also, weakened or damaged muscles will require a stronger stimulus — the intensity of the necessary current is recorded and comparisons made throughout the course of treatment.

MASSAGE

Used in conjunction with other forms of treatment to reduce inflammation, massage can have highly therapeutic qualities. It improves the local circulation, resulting in an increase in the rate at which waste products are removed from the area. There are two main types of massage:

Friction massage. When massaging the limbs, in particular the tendons, most benefit is gained from small movements concentrated in one area — the fingers press, following the line of the tissues beneath the skin. A lubricant should be used to allow the fingers to slide easily over the coat.

Mechanical massage machines. These may be hand-held units or specialized adhesive pads. The affected area of the limb should be fitted with a tube-grip stocking and the machine worked over this to prevent a skin reaction. The horse should initially be allowed to become used to a low level of vibration, which can be gradually increased. Treatment will probably be necessary three times daily, for thirty minutes per session, continued until the condition has noticeably improved.

SUPPORT

Support is an important aid in preventing excessive inflammation of an area. In extreme cases, the vet may apply a plaster cast. After cold treatments have been administered, support bandages should be used to prevent a sudden surge of blood and fluids back to the area. When bandaging for support, a wide elasticated bandage should be used over a substantial amount of padding. The bandage should extend from just below the knee or hock to the coronet. Do not bandage in the same way as when applying support bandages for exercise because the area left unbandaged between the fetlock and coronet will fill with fluid very quickly.

Pressure bandages must be removed regularly and the legs massaged to encourage healthy circulation before the bandages are replaced. The contralateral limb must always be bandaged as it will be subjected to extra strain. When applying bandages, an even pressure must be maintained and any pressure points resulting from rucks in the padding or bandage must be avoided. Bad bandaging can cause more problems than it solves.

ANTI-INFLAMMATORY DRUGS

When an area of tissue becomes damaged, a chemical known as arachidonic acid is released. This is then acted on by an enzyme called cyclo-oxygenase. The result of this interaction is the conversion of arachidonic acid into prostaglandins, the chemicals which cause the symptoms of heat, pain and swelling and also increase the sensitivity of pain receptors in the area.

Anti-inflammatory drugs which may be administered to reduce the painful effects of inflammation can be divided into two main groups; corticosteroids and non-steroidal anti-inflammatories.

Corticosteroids

Cortisol, a natural compound, was originally used in anti-inflammatory corticosteroids, but it is now more common for synthetic corticosteroids to be used. The exact manner in which these drugs act on inflammation is not definitely known, but it is considered that they act within the nuclei of the affected cells, causing an alteration to the production of proteins. Their anti-inflammatory effects include:

Stabilizing cell membranes (reducing release of damaging enzymes).

Inhibiting prostaglandin release.

Inhibiting white blood cell migration.

Reducing fibrosis — fibrin deposition.

Reducing fluid accumulation.

However, since they inhibit the healing process and suppress the immune response, they should not be used in open wounds or in the presence of infection.

Corticosteroids may be injected directly into the inflamed area (for example, into a joint) or administered intravenously. Generally, a single dose can be given without serious side effects, but prolonged treatment can be dangerous.

Non-steroidal anti-inflammatory drugs

These drugs are chemically unrelated to cortisol, being of a different chemical structure.

The non-steroidal drugs in use include the well known phenylbutazone (bute) and less well known meclofenamic acid, flunixin meglamine and naproxen. These drugs act by neutralizing the enzyme cyclo-oxygenase — without this chemical catalyst the arachidonic acid cannot be converted into prostaglandins, so the signs of inflammation will subside.

All drugs should be administered under veterinary advice as all have side-effects and the random use of them, particularly if given in too large a dosage, can have serious long-term effects. The subject of drugs and their effect on the horse is discussed more fully in another book in this series. *The Horse: Physiology.*

BLISTERING AND FIRING

These so-called 'therapies' have become less common, indeed firing is now illegal in the UK.

Blisters involve the application of an irritant substance such as mercuric iodide which causes inflammation and blistering. The idea behind them is that circulation will be improved to bring about healing, thus benefiting the damaged tendons, and that the resultant scar tissue will provide a strengthened support to the area.

Firing was supposed to produce the same results — the skin being pierced either in parallel lines (line firing) or in a matrix of dots (pin firing), by a red-hot iron. Research proved that firing did not enhance the healing process; in fact it hindered it and caused unnecessary suffering to the horse.

Although firing is illegal, some still advocate the use of blisters and it is the responsibility of the horse owner to decide whether or not to subject the horse to further discomfort, particularly when so many effective, non-irritant, analgesic therapies are available.

RECOVERY AND REHABILITATION

After any injury or illness there will be the need for a period of recovery and rehabilitation, the duration and nature of which will depend upon the severity of the condition. Post-operative recovery is obviously a specialist subject requiring the expertise of the veterinary team and the clinic facilities.

The object of rehabilitation is to restore to normality the injured tissue and/or bone through repair and re-education (encouraging the restored tissue and attendant structures to function correctly). The repair process may be aided by physiotherapy — the selective use of machines will promote healing and reduce pain.

Traditionally, the majority of horses are turned away to rest immediately after injury has occurred — if the injury is causing discomfort, it will lead to the horse moving in an unbalanced way to compensate. This movement may well become established, developing an uneven gait and muscular build-up which will probably be maintained upon full recovery. As the horse is constantly moving out of balance the old injury is likely to recur or indeed, a new injury may result. Correct rehabilitation before the horse is turned away to rest can greatly improve the chances of a full and balanced recovery, resulting in prolonged soundness. Therefore, during treatment and rehabilitation the physiotherapist, vet and owner will need to work closely together, monitoring the horse's reaction to treatment, and his progress. When the vet and physiotherapist are in agreement, re-education can commence.

Swimming, which may be included in the rehabilitation programme, is very useful as the horse's limbs bear no weight. However, care must be taken to ensure that each limb is used evenly to promote even muscular development. The heart-rate monitor should be used as the horse may easily become stressed if unused to swimming. Walking in water, particularly against a current, is also very beneficial. The sea is ideal, otherwise a safe stream or wading area at a pool can be used.

Straight line work at the walk on long-reins can, if carried out properly, help to even out muscular imbalances. Circle work would exert too much strain on the muscles and joints.

Once a high level of recovery has been achieved, basic ridden schooling can supple and strengthen muscles as well as helping to improve balance. Steady work over raised poles improves rhythm and tempo whilst encouraging the horse to flex his joints effectively. At the riding stage of the rehabilitation programme, it is important to appreciate that correct shoeing, bitting, care of teeth and saddle fitting will all affect the horse's chances of staying in balance.

CONCLUSION

As a result of hereditary, conformational or physiological factors, some horses will always be prone to unsoundness. However, the more their handlers understand about the underlying problems and inherent risks, the better their chances of avoiding or minimizing problems.

This principle holds true in essence for *all* horses — it is the responsibility of everyone who rides or cares for them to try to promote their long-term soundness by improving their own understanding of the factors involved. In practice, the fundamentals can be summarized thus:

Ensuring that, through good and regular farriery, the optimum foot balance and pastern/foot axis are maintained.

Undertaking a fittening and work programme appropriate to the individual horse and avoiding work which entails excessive jarring and concussion.

Being observant — knowing what is normal and what is not, and taking abnormalities as early warning signs and acting upon them.

Finally, in addition to the moral considerations of welfare, it does no harm to remind ourselves that promoting soundness in the horse is very much in the owner's interests — the old saying 'No foot, no horse' remains as true as ever.

INDEX

Page numbers in *italics* refer to figures

124